This is to everyone who
to many to mention bu

FOREWORD

This idea first started with a simple conversation. It was with a fellow adult. Yes, I am an adult, although I admit don't always act like one. I told this person about my latest stand-up comedy gig and how great it was. He complimented me and told me that "one day, you'll make it."

The next day I was talking to someone about a band who were on my t-shirt. They asked who they were, and I explained, probably in painstaking detail, how kick-ass rock awesome they were, how great their songs are, how their stagecraft is top drawer and how seeing them live brings joy to the audience. Again, the response was, "they sound great. It's so difficult to make it these days. These guys sound like they deserve to make it."

It dawned on me. That band *have* made it. And hence, so have I. Both this band and I, do what we love. We get to perform regularly, sometimes to large audiences. When performing, members of the audience are lost in the show. Be it laughing, cheering, whooping or singing along, they are stuck in the moment. Thoughts of mortgage rates, divorce bills, the affair you are having and the stress of secrecy, the affair you think your spouse is having with her personal trainer, monetary issues which nobody else knows about, wedding guest lists, car problems, that MOT you won't pass. These thoughts are temporarily forgotten about. The audience are living in the present; you know the place all these thousands of self-development books tell you to aim for. Right in the moment. There could be nothing but the performance and pure joy in the room.

Us, as entertainers have supplied that moment. Made it from imagination, talent and will.

Have we "made it"?

Absolutely we have.

As I am writing this, the world is nuts. And our wellbeing is vital. It must be a priority. Your own landing must be swept before you help look after someone else, after all.

Being creative has an overall effect on our wellbeing. And of course, in the cycle, people tend to be most creative when they are in a good mood. But for us to be more creative, we need to feel inspired in the first place. In a world full of narcissism, lies, pandemics, Piers Morgan, Katie Hopkins and conspiracy theories we are so busy being angry and can sometimes forget what makes us feel truly alive.

Working with kids I regularly ask them what they want to be when they grow up and they reply that they want to be youtubers. Why? Because they make millions of pounds, they say. They go on and tell me they want to be on *YouTube* or *Tik-Tok* and have millions of followers and hence rake in the cash. I then ask why they want millions of pounds and they can't really answer. Well, not a real answer anyway. A shrug isn't an answer unless you're a teenager or a despondent politician. Some of the kids talk about music. Yeah! Boom, music to my ears. They want to be in a band they tell me. Yeah, boom. Great news. I ask them why? To be rich, they say. To have millions of followers and rake in the cash. The pattern is a clear one. And surely, it's going to lead to confusion, disappointment and above all failure. Which has its own consequences.

Does this culture of fame and fortune need to be dismantled? I believe so, but that's not an easy task. So, let's at least question it? The culture that youtubers, The X-Factor, The Voice, reality television like Love Island and Big Brother have contributed to is not a healthy one, I'm sure most would agree. Unless you are the executive producer of the show in question or Gemma Collins.

The purpose of this movement and book INSPIRE is to simply inspire people to be more creative. Why? Because it's human nature, that's why.

Is the end goal to swim in your pool of hundred-dollar bills like Scrooge McDuck and have more cars than Jason Kay from Jamiroquai? If so, I can't help you. But if the journey is that of the end goal, then let's make that journey worth travelling.

Think about it. Creativity provides inspiration, inspiration provides creativity and makes the world a better place to live. And above all makes you feel good. And *if* you are lucky, makes other people feel good. So surely doing or making something is worth it.

This book will share techniques and discussions on being creative. It will explore the how and the why people make awesome music. It may explain the journey through that stray neurone giving you the loose idea for the album release, book launch or the moment of pride when the idea smashed through the finish line.

I will look and share techniques on how to feel more inspired, how to maximise conditions for creativity and will share from the experts in their field, tales of inspiration.

If this project helps inspire one person to walk on to that stage, lose weight, run a marathon, take up acting, do more steps, paint that wall, play the recorder, finish that novel they started in 1986 or simply be a better person than yesterday, then my job is done.

And hopefully, like the great people who have gone before us we, ourselves will inspire others with our work.

Inspiring someone to create something new is one of the most powerful tools we all own. And the world will surely be a better place than how we found it.

INTRODUCTION

So, why are you doing this? Ask yourself this question over and over and over again. After all, *why* is the most important question to be asked and sometimes it is the one that is ignored. It's easier to focus on the how. The *how* needs to be discussed, but the *why* is the key. The *why* must be continually asked, year after year, tour after tour, release after release.

But let us not go ahead of ourselves. First let's ask this question straight up. Why are you doing this? It might be a waste of time, right?

I mean, let's be honest. Do you really want to spend time justifying to the other members of the group that this song with a bit of development and teamwork could be a classic?

The rehearsal will just be half an hour playing and two hours faffing, right? And then discussions about the album release and the tour will inevitably end up in an argument. That joint double-headliner will be discussed again, no doubt. Whose responsibility is it to bring the breakables? Is it worth getting the merchandise sorted? And how can you stop the singer from turning up late? Maybe he could help with the drum kit on and off the stage, even just once?

Do we really want to spend the extra money on the back print of the t-shirt? What do you mean the van needs a MOT? Who is going to pay for that? The record label? Yeah, right. Whose responsibility is it to get the new single out to the networks? Maybe they should slack the PR woman off, she's a bit on the rubbish side, right?

Maybe it was would be easier to let it slide. Watch the game - it's the *Champions League* after all and if you're being honest, you're a bit tired. You work hard, right? You deserve a break, get your feet up and maybe open a can of lager and get on your comfortable joggers with the tea stain on the left-hand side. You've not watched *Emmerdale* or *Coronation Street* for years. Maybe it will be good to catch up with the Dingles or to see if Steve McDonald is looking visibly older. Is Jim still in *Neighbours*? Who's in charge of the Queen Vic now? Maybe I'll sit here and see.

Or maybe a little gaming instead? Your PS4 is sitting there. Imagine that, jump on. Become the greatest football manager in the world, get good enough to get a *YouTube* channel, make millions.

In fact, you only have three more episodes of that series to watch on *Netflix*. You know, the one with the placid but dangerous handsome but tired cop and the beautiful Swedish woman who craves power and politics more than life. Three more episodes, that's all. And then you are caught up. You can give it a break. Or start the next season, maybe?

It would take a phone call, not even that – a text message. SORRY GUYS, NOT FEELING IT TONIGHT. You could even say you were self-isolating. Anyway, after last year's pandemic is it worth getting back on the road just for it to be cancelled again? Maybe it was a sign, an omen. A sign from God to tell you to pack it in, to let it go. To grow up. To be like most other people. To get that boxset watched. To see if that blond bombshell gets her comeuppance. To see what manner of disaster occurs in Roy's Cafe.

The phone is on the arm of your chair, next to the remote control. There's a beer in the fridge. You pick up the remote then look up, past your television and your PS4 sitting idly. Past these is a shelf, which is holding a fraction of your record collection.

You walk over to it, placing your finger on the surface and gently pulling free the centre vinyl. It shows a monster/robot thing attacking the people of Earth. You slide it back and look at the cover of the next one showing a toddler swimming, a dollar bit floating in front. You continue looking through the covers, from Queen to Nirvana, Led Zeppelin to Pearl Jam, Miles Davis to Metallica, Stevie Wonder to Soundgarden.

These are not bodies of work for you to appreciate. They are not slices of popular culture for you to dissect, evaluate, discuss and compare. These are *memories.* You remember asking your Mum who was playing on her record player when *Bring Back Leroy Brown* was airing through your home. You remember getting home from *Our Price* with Metallica's *Master of Puppets* and playing it relentlessly. Memories of the sun beaming through the sky when Chris Cornell introduced *Jesus Christ Pose*, watching Eddie Vedder drink his bottle of red wine. Memories flood back of watching Keith Moon, Ginger Baker, John Bonham, transfixed by what these superhumans could do. It doesn't matter how long you have inhabited this small planet of ours. It may be memories of *The Old Grey Whistle Test* or *Top of the Pops*; it may be watching some pop-punk on *Kerrang TV* or *MTV.* Your memories may suddenly take you back to that 1985 day when you watched Freddie take on the world, or when you watched Black Sabbath for the first time in that field surrounded by 70 000 like-minded people. You will always remember the feeling of joy when Angus Young took to the stage in his school uniform wielding his guitar like a medieval knight with his lance. When the curtain dropped on Aerosmith's *Get a Grip Tour* and Steven Tyler resembled the child-snatcher from *Chitty Chitty Bang Bang*, clutching the mic stand and hitting notes that humans shouldn't be able to reach. Remember when you were told over the tannoy that "You wanted the best, you got the best", just before KISS took to the stage. The adrenalin was pumping. You had the plastic pint in your hand and nothing else in the entire planet mattered at that moment in time. You remember when your heart lifted with pride when Steve Harris pointed his bass guitar to you and snarled the chorus of *Bring Your Daughter to the Slaughter*, when Rachel Bolan sang *Psycho Therapy*, when Fish began the opening verse of *Vigil in The Wilderness of Mirrors* from inside the crowd. I will always remember watching Bruce Springsteen sing *Thunder Road* and wondering why it wasn't classed as the 8th Wonder of the World.

Putting the vinyl back, you return to your sofa, pick up the remote control and switch off your television.

It's time to make some music. It's time to make memories and to create something that no-one has seen or heard before.

It's time to have an impact on someone, somewhere. You may not know who or where. But an impact could be made. It could change someone's whole life or simply alter their mood for three minutes. It may inspire someone to turn into a mega superstar or help them re-connect an emotion from a long time ago, re-kindle that memory nearly faded, remind someone to make a phone call, send a text message, give someone a hug and remind them the world is actually a good place to be.

Switching off your television may alter the course of history. The power-hungry politician or the barman at the *Rovers Return* can wait. It's time to make a difference.

Do not die with music still in you.

CHAPTER 1: PASS THE BATON

The year 2020 sucked. It really did. That statement was undeniable. Brexit was a mess, riots and protests filled our screens. Two grey-haired men in America squabbled, one claiming he would be a better leader, the other claiming that he was the most suited person for the job in the world who ever and would ever live. And of course, a little virus called Covid-19 took the limelight and grabbed everyone's attention. Gemma Collins must have been fuming with the ability of this little bastard to get all the headlines. The news was filled with doom, gloom and negativity. But that's sells, right? So, it wasn't really a surprise. We have been conditioned to watch this all on our screens - and if you are like me sometimes 24 hours a day on every platform imaginable. It shouldn't be called news. Is it new? Nope, because I've seen the same headlines 47 times so far and when it says *Breaking News*, it doesn't actually mean *breaking*. It means *repeating*. Repeating news. Groundhog Day headlines. And yes, the information comes from the North, East, West and South, but let's call it what it is. WWWT. What went wrong today? What went wrong today? The virus. What went wrong today? The Government. What went wrong today? Energy companies, natural disasters, global warming, racism, war, power struggles, droughts, floods, fires, deaths, bankruptcy, Brexit, independence, murder, violence, greed, Coldplay. Justin Bieber.

And then there is our social media feed. Man, oh man. Opinions and opinions. No-one really cares about someone else's opinion, right? If I'm eating a take-away pizza in my boxer shorts and watching *Toy Story 3* whilst crying into my Vegetarian Hot as Woody, Buzz and the gang fall down a trash compacter, I don't give a shit if it got 8 out of 10 on *Rotten Tomatoes* or Jeanine said that it wasn't as good as the first one and they should have quit making them after the second outing. I actually give less of a shit that someone in Co-op didn't wear a mask, or that someone's boyfriend is a bastard and we should block them, or that your ex-partner hasn't picked up your kids as he promised and he's a bastard and needs to take responsibility as an adult and a father. Nope. Sorry. I couldn't give a shit. At all. Nobody really does. Shits given, absolutely none.

But that's the issue. We then feel we *should* give a shit. We feel the need to comment or argue. Don't get me wrong, I love the socials, and I enjoy seeing what people are up to, what albums people are listening to or hearing how people are getting on with their day. It can be uplifting or calming or simply nice. But unfortunately, it's poisoned by anger. And hate. And annoying people who tell me I'm a fool if I don't think David Ike is right and the mainstream media is a weapon for the Illuminati. And that weird bird-faced woman who was once on *The Apprentice* is in this case right, or immigrants don't want us to use the term Christmas trees or other nasty untruths designed to rile people up and spread nastiness quicker than the truth can halt it.

We need to use these information tools better. Let's use them for discovery, for joy, creativity, inspiration. For love and happiness. Let's be hitting that thumbs up button more often than pressing that angry face button. These devices should bring a smile to your face and result in you listening to an album or watching a film or reading a book or humming a song or finding the book that the quote has been lifted from. Filled with gratitude to the people who recommended that previously undiscovered EP and you thanking them for the discovery. It can't be solely used for being annoyed about someone's opinion or writing "What's Wrong Hun? X" on someone's wall, desperately hoping they don't get in a conversation about their ex and his/her inability to pick up their kids.

So come on peoples, let's start the revolution. Let's pick up your phone, click on *Facebook* or *Instagram* or *Twitter* (I'm old, these are the only ones I know) and ask the questions '"What am I going to discover today? What's going to inspire me?"

Because life's too short to worry about your sister's flatmate's cousin's affair with the kid's social worker. Or lose sleep over some prick jumping on a group and starting an argument, for the only reason that everyone else in their real world will agree with them for an easy life.

Let the revolution begin.

Let's get inspired.

***

So, what is meant by inspiration?

The definition to inspire is *to excite, encourage, or breathe life into.* ***Inspire*** *comes from the Latin word that* means *to inflame or to blow in to. When you* ***inspire*** *something, it is as if you are blowing air over a low flame to make it grow.*

I know this as I stole it straight from the internet, but it seems pretty accurate to me. Not the flame bit, that makes no sense, but the excite, encourage and breathing life bit. And when you are feeling this way, your heart pumping, you feel excited and alive, life is bloody ace. This is what we need more of. Not a picture of someone's legs on a sunbed making you feel jealous. Not jealous of their legs but jealous of their Pina Colada they have taken hours to balance to get in the photo.

The feeling of being inspired. You know what this is? It's the feeling I get when I watch the *Rocky* movies. (Maybe not the 5th one but I can't swear by that.) When Sly Stallone gets back up off the floor, when Mickey tells him he can do it, when he and Apollo dance on the ocean like a pair of star-crossed lovers. When he runs up the stairs in Philadelphia, when he solves the whole Cold War single handed. Watching these movies, I feel alive and encouraged with the world. It's the feeling I get when I look out on a beautiful day, the rolling Staffordshire landscapes, the wildlife, the sun breaking through the clouds that look like a massive fluffy unicorn/dragon hybrid. The same feeling as when I am standing with a thousand other people, watching a band storm the stage, more which I will talk about later. But after a gig or a movie, or a play, I get home and I ask the question. How can I make an impact? That, my friends is inspiration.

It doesn't matter if you are headlining Hyde Park, Download Festival, the Reading or Leeds Festivals, or Glastonbury - or if you are playing in *The Moon Under the Water* with three lonely guys and a scrappy dog for an audience (we've all been there). Ask yourself why you are there? Always the why.

If it is to make millions of pounds, add to a collection of fast cars and live in the Hollywood Hills, whilst married to a supermodel and eat Cornflakes from a breakfast bowl handmade by autistic Himalayan elves, you are probably in the wrong job. Don't get me wrong - money's great. Being rich is amazing. (This is an assumption as I am not rich, never been rich and will probably never be rich.) Money is brilliant, I just don't really have enough of it. However, even if I think about this statement, this is a lie. I do have enough of the green stuff. (An outdated phrase if I have ever heard one.) Yes, the bank and credit card companies love me as I pay them more interest monthly than I can afford and I don't have a swimming pool or a fast car – in fact, I don't even own a car. I live in Staffordshire and can't drive, so neither of them would be much cop anyway. But I have enough. More than enough. I eat, drink, listen to music, gig, can afford what I need and appreciate the odd take-away or two.

If money is your motivator, start a business (those pyramid-selling schemes are quite good) and go make millions. Talk shit, pretend you know what you are talking about whilst never actually *doing* anything and make the money. Or marry that really annoying fat woman who originated from reality television and has been on every single reality television programme in the history of the universe since.

Don't get me wrong, you might make money. A lot of it. If you do, good on you. Buy me a pint.

Will it make you happy? I don't know. Probably not. James Hetfield looks pretty miserable. Gene Simmons and Paul Stanley feel the need to keep on acquiring more of the readies, surely quicker than they can spend it.

But if you are spending your time on *Facebook* complaining that *Spotify* doesn't give you any money then that's not doing you any good. In these times, there realistically is no money in music. Don't think of that 0.0000000009 pence you will get from your digital royalties. It will kill you. And I'm not defending them here for the record, that's just the way it is. That's not why you are doing it. Music is too easy to get now. Long gone are the days you had to trek to *Woolworths* in Broughty Ferry to purchase *Rock Me Amadeus* by Falco on a Wednesday after school, because all ten copies would be gone by Friday. (Thursday was visiting Granny in case you ask.)

But let me tell you this. There is a reason you should play an instrument. Forget the wad of cash. You *should* do it, firstly, because it makes you happy. The feeling of that guitar or that bass hanging low should make you feel like a million dollars. (Watch out, Gene may steal you.) The feeling of sitting on your throne banging things (I know it's more complicated than that for drummers) should feel like nothing on earth. The thought of standing on the keys, or singing out loud, making your voice an instrument of the Gods should fill you with wonder. (If Bob Dylan is reading this, God's have obscure instruments too.)

If it's the creating process that makes you happy - as it should - get creative. Starting with a blank canvas and ending up with something new is simply magical. It's alchemy - plain and simple. *Bohemian Rhapsody, The Immigrant Song, Master of Puppets, Paradise City* had begun on blank canvases. Followed by one thought. Then another, then another. Imagine if that blank canvas hadn't been scribbled on. Imagine if, out of a billion billion billion (let's call it a zillion, I don't know) thoughts - that these particular five thoughts had never occurred. Possibly the electrical impulses missed the synapses and weren't received by the following neuron. Imagine for a second, would you? Imagine a world, today in fact with no Thin Lizzy, with no *Live Aid*, no Woodstock, Glastonbury or Download Festival. Songs simply exist such as *Run to The Hills, Back in Black, Tie Your Mother Down, Imagine, Enter Sandman, Detroit Rock City, Brown Sugar, Captain Beaky and His Band*. From these blank canvases, just a small idea that evolved into something that can alter moods and change lives. These songs, bands and festivals originally spawned from just one thought. And these thoughts began the process of art, which causes inspiration in itself. The circle of inspiration. All due to a firing neurone and a blank piece of paper. Oh, and probably a pen.

Creation is magic, and magic is creation. If you hear me playing the guitar, then hear Myke Gray playing it, you can understand his involves magic whist mine involves fat fingers and a poor ear. Creativity is, **"the desire to create is one of the deepest yearnings of the human soul,"** Dieter F. Uchtdorf said. I read that on a research paper on the conceptualisation of the process of thought. Actually, I read it on *Pinterest*, but it's all the same in the end.

If you enjoy the creation process because you love the audience's reaction, maybe you've got an ego bigger than Switzerland and love showing your skills, getting off with wanting people to dig your work. If that's the case, that's okay too. In fact, that's bloody great. It's not really you they've come to see and hear. It's your work. It's what you have created. With a blank canvas and that firing neurone, you have made something from nothing, and people have paid (sometimes) to see that. Pretty cool, huh? The fact that people have spent their hard-earned cash to buy your creativity is star-spangled awesome.

So, the next time you ask why, answer your own question. You ask is it really worth setting up my kit, taking these singing lessons, playing hours of scales when you just want to play the cool bit in *Sweet Child O' Mine* - think of the answer. Think of all the people who went before you. Think of what Freddie Mercury, Phil Lynott, Robert Plant, John Bonham, Bon Scott, Elvis Presley, Bruce Springsteen, Toby Jepson, Ricky Warwick have given you and given others. Think of that one person, no matter what the age who will watch you and listen to you, then re-string their guitar. Or decide the song they wrote five years ago needs completing or will ask their Mum for a drum kit or a microphone.

You are continuing the stream of musical awesomeness. When others are bitchin' about the one-way system in *Lidl,* you are creating something so powerful that in a hundred years' time, some spotty teenager may pick up the cassette (they'll be back) and listen to your work and think, "Dude – they were brilliant. You don't get music like this anymore."

So, without sounding like a *Nike* advert – go do it. Change the world. Write that song, perfect that riff, hit stuff (yes, drummers – I know you do more than that), sing that song. And go create something. And inspire someone.

If music is too easily accessible think of it that more people are listening to something you have created. You are inspiring them. And yes, you should be earning more for it but you ain't. So, take that thought of inspiring others to the bank instead. Because most of the population don't have that talent. Haven't produced that spark in somebody else (no rude jokes here).

They say Guthrie inspired Springsteen who inspired Bon Jovi who inspired Collateral.

So, this is your gift to the world. Switch off *Tipping Point* (Sorry, Ben) and go and change lives. Give someone that thought - which will produce the spark, which will produce a song or a band or a best-selling album that millions more people will listen to. Go do it. Pass the baton.

An example of seeing the baton of rock-and-roll passed down the generation is Massive. If you ever have the pleasure of catching Massive live, the show is spectacular. The amount of energy emitting from the Australian four-piece is a wonder. The last time I caught them live, I was invited to join them on stage with others for their tune *Dancefloor*. I had spent most of the day at the side of the stage as I was part of the DJ team and helping out with compering duties, so I could tell the mood of the crowd. Throughout Massive's set, literally thousands of people were dancing, smiling, rocking out and simply having a spell of joy. I caught up with Brad Marr to discuss his role in this world of music. I started off asking whom he received his baton from and the reasons he chose to spend his life in music. Who influenced the dynamite Mr Marr? And who are Massive? The last question is answered simply and with clarity. “Our brand is fun and rock n roll and fun.”

“Guns n Roses - *Appetite for Destruction*, was the first rock-and-roll album for me,” he said, “then I went down the rabbit hole of going through your parent’s records collection.

When I started a band, I didn’t have any interest in making it. I just wanted to play rock n roll with my friends, there was no ulterior motive to make money.

These days I’m motivated by working, I love to play and love to write music. So, now music is what I do. The bands that inspired me the - Guns n Roses, Sabbath, AC/DC and now music is now who I am. What I do.”

Talking to Brad about what he does and what Massive do, I mention the affect he has on the crowd. I asked him if he notices when he is on that stage how he is touching people’s lives.

“We’re good enough to get on stage and smash it. We can play the same gig 100 nights in the row and smash it. If you are having fun, the crowd are having fun too.

I don’t notice on stage, it’s still difficult to run around on stage and do what we do. Most of the time I’m on stage, my eyes are closed. Not because I don’t want to see what I’m doing, because I’m in pain.

The feeling when you get off stage, when you meet hundreds or thousands or dozens of people, depending on the size of the gig – the joy is transferred from you to them back to you. You've passed that energy on to them and they then pass it back to you. That energy is transferred back and forth, and it brings the vibe. Then when you get off the stage and you meet and greet; the vibe is there and that will never go away. Hopefully."

And he's right. I've seen Massive leave the stage after a show. The smiles on their faces just as large as the audiences. Spirits have been lifted and the relationship between band and audience is clear and recognised. "I've been in bands and with bands who take it too seriously, we've been doing it for long enough," Brad says with a smile on his face.

We chat about the business side of it, the merchandise and the promotion then Brad says, "when we get on stage, that's party time."

Brad and I talk about the meaning of success and what it means to be "successful" in this creative bubble. His answer is of no surprise, but exceptionally important as an example.

"For me, success is being able to do it and continue to do it.

If we can afford to pay our rent and be on to the road for a month, 6 months a year and without having to sacrifice the most important things in life, like family and health. If we can do that, it is success.

If in 50 years' time if I have inspired thousands of kids to play the guitar that's cool, if I've inspired a handful of people to have a good time in a pub, that's also cool for me. I don't care about legacy. When I'm 50 years old, I'll be playing a stadium or a pub, I'll still be playing regardless. My level of success is nothing to do with how many people buy the record or how many people I play to."

With the hundreds of books on the secret of success on sale and seminars on how to be successful, I think you should just go and see Massive, listen to their albums and if you can, meet up with Brad Marr. He knows his stuff.

We chat about how they cope. Bands can be stressful and like I indicated earlier in the chapter, the hassle can be the catalyst to give up and switch on the television instead. But as Mr Marr shows, if there's an obstacle, then identify it and step over it.

"We don't practice, the Australia guys live 10 hours apart, so technically we are a Dropbox band. The more rock n roll stuff is Ben, the more melodic stuff is me. You must have a little bit of leadership, yes but we work together well. Then for 3 or 4 days we get in the studio, same as before a tour, and we make sure we are up to scratch.

There are no fights, because we don't see each other. You can handle someone's negative attitude for 3 or 4 weeks."

Lastly, I ask Brad who inspires him these days. "I don't look at music anymore and think are they famous? Are they in an indie band? It's just all music to me. Whether they are famous or not doesn't matter. If it's good, it inspires me."

Talking to Massive's Brad Marr was interesting as every time I have seen them live, which is a few, I can sense the attitude and energy in each performance. I next chatted to another friend of mine, a man whom I first met when I was queuing up for his autograph in *Tower Records* in 1995 when he was the guitarist for Little Angels. This was roughly the same time I watched him share the stage with Van Halen. Yeah, pretty rad or what? In recent years, I know Bruce Dickinson from a slightly different angle. I was introduced to him by Toby Jepson and Dave Kemp in Brighton when I was supporting Wayward Sons and recently; I worked closely with him in the Master's Degree in Music Enterprise I completed.

Bruce has been there, done that, bought the t-shirt, then repeated. He now runs *WaterBear College of Music* and is a true inspiration for every artist who meets him. A man who has lived every teenage dream, Bruce now is very reflective in his approach to success. A truly creative mind and a huge inspiration I catch up with him and begin by asking him what success means to him. Is it to "make it" in a band?

"The idea of making it is total illusion," Bruce says. "Instead of selling 20 tickets, you sell 200. It's the same thing, just condensed. But so are your problems, that's why you get high-profile suicides and peoples live falling apart in the public eye. It doesn't make you happier. Just multiplies the pressure. All success is all human activities condensed, so all more aggravation condensed.

People have understood human happiness for thousands of years. Don't stress too much, live in the moment and be nice to people.

It is a big monkey on your back - chasing recognition, the same amount of people who like you will dislike you and be vocal about it. And if you are attracted to one, you will be exposed to the other."

I've had many chats with Bruce over the past few years and his philosophy comes from many different places. His influences include Eckart Tolle and Wayne Dyer, but a lot of what Bruce says comes from first-hand experience. I ask him about this.

"You can be forever running to the end of the rainbow to look for the gold. You may even earn a lot of money - then you are just going to get the tax bill. It's all about attachment. If you are attached to an outcome, then there is a huge risk it may not happen."

Bruce is right. If you desire fame and fortune and it doesn't come, then you may feel crushed. And as Bruce says, it's an outcome that has no endpoint.

"Accept that something might happen, but it may be different. It may open the doors for something else."

I ask him if he would rather be remembered for being one of the greatest guitarists from my generation or remembered for starting off *WaterBear College* and hence influencing and helping thousands of musicians. "None of them," he says, "I'd like to be forgotten about or remembered for spreading positivity. I would like to tread fairly lightly on the earth and spread good vibes instead of negativity."

Like many times with Bruce, I talk about getting his autograph or asking him how it felt on tour with Van Halen, but the conversation ends up with laughter and tales of fishing. I ask him about the fishing. To Bruce it's pretty simple. "Everyone needs to meditate and bring yourself in the moment, so I do a lot of meditation. When you are a mile out at sea and your phone's off, it puts you in the moment.

Everybody is looking for that time when time stands still. In fishing, you are looking for that difficult fish and chasing the one or two moments." Bruce fished in Russia for seven days, twelve hours a day and didn't catch anything.

"We all feel inspired, in spirit. That moment time stands still, and it feels like you are connected to the centre of the earth."

Bruce tells me about a pod of porpoises he discovered the day before in Brighton, his love of nature and discovery evident. Bruce's philosophy is inspiring and contagious. I ask him how he got into it and what inspired him.

My parents had a great attitude to life, not particularly materialistic, work to live, not the other way around. They designed a good life," he tells me. "When we were in school, we were in a jazz band, a big band, and the guy who conducted that had high musical standards. Tony Turner conducted it; he was influential. He had such high musical standards. This is where I met Mark Plunkett. I watched some old footage on Facebook of us. I was surprised at how good it was. This was all down to his high standards. That musical discipline was drilled into us and that has been useful and been reinforced since."

Seeing and hearing Bruce playing and seeing first-hand how he runs the college, these high standards are evident. He continues, "with the Little Angels, our manager understood the totality of being in a band and was a big part of Little Angels. I learned a lot from him. It was a big time with all the lads in the band, you realised that things you dreamt of were turning into reality and that is big."

Bruce knows probably more about the UK Rock music scene that any living soul, but more importantly to me, he shares his knowledge of the scene together with his personal experience and philosophy. He is a wise man indeed. He's like the Morgan Freeman of the music world. But plays a meaner guitar.

I also caught up about all things inspirational and motivational with Nic Wastell. Nic, is quality through and through. Again, like Bruce, Nic is a rock star's rock star. With the past successes of Chrome Molly and the present successes with Wayward Sons, Nic has seen the working of the rock music circuit for decades.

I was lucky enough to spent two weeks on tour with Nic, when I was supporting Wayward Sons, and if the James

Bond franchise requested a silver fox who could play a funky bass and wore shoes as sparkly as his personality Wastell would be their man. His energy on stage is magnetic, hence his "flea on speed" tag. The only downside to Nic is that he refers to me as 'O-Mally'. My mother would kill him if he wasn't such a charmer.

Talking of passing the baton, I ask the flea on speed who inspired him.

"Inspiration is a massive thing. I was always into music, I was the music kid in the family, always listening to it, singing. My nan bought Beatles records, so from the age of 2 or 3, I listened to them. I was two years old when *Hard Day's Night* came out. I can remember dancing and singing the songs.

I can remember my Nan dancing and singing the songs which was brilliant as she was the nan who cooked and cleaned, but every now and then she sang *I Should Have Known Better* and danced around the room with me, so to me, it had a magic to it.

At the age of 9, I fell in love with Slade. It was everything. I'm still a massive fan of them. I'm an expert, been to conventions and all sorts. That was the first band I saw when I was 14. I'd started playing guitar by then. I was a bit small, a bit of a gobshite, I know that's hard to believe." (I know Nic, it's not)

"I realised you could be cool. The kids who played guitar were cool. It was a rugby school I went to, but I was shit at rugby. There was the rugby lot. Then there was an ocean of bland people, and then there was a small group like me, that even the rugby players liked - who could play a tune and hold their own in a conversation about Hawkwind. And I thought that's for me. I love all that - it became your identity then."

I think of Nic's Nan dancing around the kitchen and compare her in my mind's eye to Nic on that stage, leaping around the stage like Leo Sayer on cocaine.

"When younger, the other bands didn't move, didn't engage, didn't talk to the audience. I think back to all the bands I loved. In particular, Slade - all of them were doing something. The stage looked alive. Off the ball is just as important as what you do on it!

But the energy, I rehearse like that. I always play full throttle; I can't see the point in staying still in rehearsal, then trying to leap around."

"I still put my heart and soul into it. We always put our heart and soul into playing. If we are going to put an album out – everything is important. If we're going to do a show, let's do an hour and a half instead of 50 minutes That kind of constant pushing is a must."

Nic then reminds me of the Bad News story. When the comedy outfit – Rick Mayell, Nigel Planer, Peter Richardson, Ade Edmondson and Alan Metcalfe played *Monster of Rock Festival*, Rik Mayall rehearsed for two weeks sitting down. When the soundcheck finally started he realised he couldn't play standing up, hence he came on in a wheelchair.

"In rehearsals always go full-throttle and get the others to do it as well."

I ask about success and what it means to Mr Wastell. The only man in history who has played on *both Stonedeaf Festival* dates, a man who has toured the world with Alice Cooper and Ozzy Osbourne and is still pounding the boards with The Sons.

"Punk rock was an alien species when I was eighteen or nineteen. It wasn't for normal people. Normal people didn't want to know about it. Parents didn't want to know about it. We were just freaks. So, your peer group, fans and other bands - that was just magical. You just wanted to be successful in that realm. You didn't really want grannies and grandads to like you, because that would kind of mean you were a bit shit."

Everything now is about the cult of celebrity; everyone has to know about it. They feel they have got to do that or its failure."

It is uncanny that Nic and Bruce's sentiments on this are identical. Both wise, talented, modest rock stars can't be wrong, right? He continues, "we just had to be accepted in the rock world, and it still amazes me to this day when you say to someone what band you've been in. Chrome Molly? 99% of people shake their head and say nope, never heard of them. But if someone's into rock, they say, really!!

It has to be fun; I can't think of any shows that weren't fun.

With Chrome Molly we looked at places locally, then once we got the traction locally, we looked at how we could play the *Marquee*. Even if we just played it once as eighteenth on the bill, we would be happy because we played the *Marquee*. And that was another achievement for us, we always had something to aim for.

We never thought about money, we thought - if we could be a *Marquee* band, once we've played it once – we might be a *Marquee* support band. Your horizons were never aimed at *Wembley Arena*, they were always can we be a *Marquee* support band? Then after 18 supports, the guy was like – I've got a quiet Monday in a few weeks, I'll put you in as a headliner. You may get 50 or 60 in. We got about 90 in. when are you coming back, they asked. We're now *a Marquee* band!

That was enough for us for a while, we were only doing that for a year or so until we thought, what next could we do? Do you think we could play a bigger place?"

If you want advice, Nic is the man in the know.

"The first time you try something new you are going to sound shit and be shit, so you try to make it so no one is around.

On the Alice Cooper tour the tour we opened, one time we walked onto the stage at Wembley Arena, "Fucking hell,' I said, "I don't know if I can do this." I felt like a fraud."

Feeling like a fraud? Exactly my feelings supporting Wayward Sons. Bizarre? Not really, as I will discuss in later chapters.

Nic continues talking about the European Leg supporting Alice. "Lads be careful they might not like us; it may be 6 or 7 songs until we get a reaction. The lights went down and there was a massive cheer – they went nuts. It was the best feeling ever."

Every milestone is special in its way. The first *Marquee* support, the first *Hammersmith Apollo* or *Odeon* as it was, first big support. Supporting Ozzy."

Nic reminisces. "He came in the dressing room, 'Thank fuck we have a fucking British band for a change.'

He had tracksuit bottoms on, 'I fucking love British bands I do', he mumbled. It was surreal.

Lemmy saying, 'I really enjoyed your gig man,' was another milestone in my life."

Nic and I talk about fame and fortune. To me, and anybody else in the industry, Nic Wastell has succeeded in the music world. So, what is success, I ask him.

"It's not about being a rock star. Do you get off with doing this? Is it fun? If it isn't fun, do something else.

If literally, you could make more money selling t-shirts on *Amazon*."

There was a period when I liked it less, I didn't want to play anymore. It was soul-destroying playing to twelve people and putting your heart and soul in it, especially when you've played to hundreds and hundreds.

My advice for other bands - Do it. I found an identity in music, but whatever it is you want to do, just do it. If the *Download Festival* had gone ahead, it would have been two days before my 58th birthday. I've never before played on that stage, so if you told me when I was 30, in 28 years nothing much would happen but then you would be opening the main stage at *Download*, I would be in hysterics for days.

And it's not about the gear. We have bands supporting us and so many times their gear was amazing. We thought 'Bastards, look at that gear – they'll blow us to pieces but time after time that's all they got. It's the fundamentals. You must put yourself in the position of the people who are watching you. Unless you are amazing at standing there, like *Oasis* who can make that work for them.

Looking at it back from now, if you really want to do this … don't give up."

He's right, you know. Many 58-year-olds will be watching *The Antiques Roadshow* and drinking Horlicks. Nic is preparing to open up the main stage at the *Download Festival.*

"It's what Ozzy Osbourne once said to me – 'stick at it, whatever you do guys, fucking stick at it.'"

Being 58 has its merits. "I would have been stressed if I got to (*Download*) at 28, cause everything you do to that point is to determine if you can make a living from this or having to get a real job. But with hindsight, now I can enjoy it. I don't have to worry about making a living from it, I've got a family, a house, I've got a family and haven't got holes in my jeans anymore. So, if it all goes away tomorrow there's a whole world, I can stay in. I can look at it and say - I never thought this would happen.

We rehearse like we meant it.

There's a danger you can talk yourself out of this industry because you can't be David Bowie or can't be Paul McCartney. It's like you can count on 2 hands people of that stature."

Passing the baton can go two ways. Like an equilibrium reaction. Nic tells me that Toby Jepson went to see Chrome Molly when he was sixteen or seventeen. So, in a way, Nic and company influenced Toby. You see how inspiration works, escalates and escalates. It's just beautiful, isn't it?

.

CHAPTER 2: BE THAT CHANGE (and *how* to get motivated)

All this talk about inspiration is great and everything, but how do you actually *get* some motivation? How can you walk past that computer console, that remote control, ignore the text to go for a quick sneaky pint which may lead to four or five (or eight or nine, we've all been there, right?) and instead play these scales or sit and focus on some lyrics that you promised to do yesterday?

Well, if you read the literature out there on self-motivation, self-help, self-control they will give you mantras to use, give you phrases like 'your actions will produce your results' and 'the pain of suffering is always bigger than the pain of regret' or Da Vinci's banger, "one can have no smaller or greater mastery than mastery of oneself." And that dude knew his vegetables. His knowledge and wisdom were both pretty rad.

But what do these quotes mean? I once repeated the phrase to myself, "go find your damn clock!" over and over after reading a book. The next day I had forgotten what it meant. You see these phrases are an excellent way to motivate yourself *once* motivated but in truth they have about as much longevity as *Police Academy 5*. (I do recommend 1-4 though, that Mahoney, what a cheeky fellow he is.)

Thoughts create feelings which drive actions which produce results. So, these mantras alone may change your action but unless they alter your feelings, these actions will probably be changed for a short period of time. It's about longevity as well as inspiration.

There are a few things however, that can certainly help motivate yourself and I will explain them in this chapter.

Again, I state *help,* as you are the driver in this. They work for me, 100% I can tell you. For example, it's now 6.20am and I'm sitting, happily typing this. I thought about walking downstairs, switching on *Good Morning Britain* with a brew and watching Susanna Reid argue with Piers Morgan. Within five minutes I would be distracted by Susanna Reid's beauty or by Piers Morgan annoying quiffy hairstyle, then watch him shouting at a guest, then get annoyed at him shouting at the same guest, then I would switch off the telly with a sigh. I know this will happen, but I can't help myself. Maybe Ben Shephard's on instead, or maybe I'll miss out of some hilarities from Kate Garraway. However, the real reason, and this is most normal, is I just want to sit on my arse and relax. Even though I hate myself for it.

So, some of these techniques may work for you, some won't. But give them a chance. Remember the first time you heard Metallica's *Death Magnetic* album, or the first episode of *Breaking Bad.* 'Right,' you thought. 'This isn't great.' But you got hooked, right? Exactly. (Note: I didn't use *Lulu* by Lou Reed and Metallica as an example here).

The first thing is a to-do-list. Now this sounds simple, you say. For this I use a pen and a highlighter. I don't type it on my computer but use paper. The highlighter can be any colour; however, I recommend pink for no reason whatsoever. Many books and gurus say this should be done in the past tense, as in you've already done these things – but I don't bother with that. This is your choice, see what works for you.

Why this list works is that when you achieve a task - and believe me, it could be simple – 1) Wake up by 7am. 2) Have a shower 3) Set up equipment 4) Switch phone off – and once you achieve them, you highlight them which then makes you feel good. When these jobs are done and marked off, this gives you that physical feeling of satisfaction. This physical feeling really matters (a point I will get to later).

Getting up early in the morning is vital and is my second point. Me, personally I do my best work first thing in the morning. I would love to talk about neuro-cortex connections and the psychology of sleep, the physiology of the waking brain and the inner workings of the anterior cingulate cortex in relation to the dorsolateral prefrontal cortex, but in truth by midday, I get a bit tired and get distracted by *Homes Under The Hammer, News* and the weather for the twenty-fifth time that day.

Also, if you wake up without smashing the snooze button a hundred times you reward yourself. The first thing on the list can be ticked off with that pink highlighter. Instant motivation! And again, that striking off a thing in your list feels good, produces some chemicals and makes you feel even more motivated.

Another thing I do is have set my alarm and link it to a song. A song which anchors you in a great mood (I will talk about anchors later). This is when you can laugh at me and finally realise that I'm about as cool as a Geography teacher who thinks he's a wild trend-setter by not wearing socks with his loafers or wearing the Tasmanian Devil on his tie. I wake up with either Huey Lewis and The News's *Fore*, Chicago *2* or *16*, Aerosmith's *Pump* or the Red Hot Chili Peppers *Freaky Styley*. I used to wake up with the radio but hearing about an explosion in Libya or a car-accident in North London didn't set up my day the way I wanted it to. Funny that, eh? I just don't understand why it took me twenty-years to figure this gem out.

Many of these 'gurus' or experts (my disclaimer here is I am neither. I'm just a dude at his best place in life with much trial and error and have thankfully discovered what works for me) look at visualisation as a technique. See it and believe it etc. For example, if you know the day is going to be shit, it's going to be shit. If you imagine yourself playing in front of thousands of screaming fans, you will be. I don't know. I've visualised my wedding day - with Belinda Carlisle, singing Heaven Can Wait with Maiden at Donnington and fighting alongside Tony Stark and Rocket Raccoon. But maybe I digress. For me, I try not to visualise what *could* go wrong. We all know the people like Eeyore who *know* that things are going to go wrong and when they do they hit you with the told-you-so line that just makes you want to walk away and scream. Instead, try to visualise the *feelings* you may get when you walk on that stage, or get that cheer and try to find that emotion. Once you have found it, this may motivate you to get prepared, get motivated and get on with your work instead of procrastinating. Because that feeling felt good, right? And it could be multiplied by a hundred. Again, this is linked to anchoring which I will talk about later as it's a powerful tool indeed.

All these techniques take work, but eventually you will feel more motivated. Feeling more motivated, you will feel inspired. And hence inspire others. And this is the crux. Although based very much on bands, inspiring others isn't just standing on that stage looking star-spangled awesome and producing ass-crunching great tunes. You will change others' lives by smiling, by that twinkle in the eye, a small gesture, a kind word.

Most people will walk down the street and you won't even see them. Mr Cellophane. And they won't see you. But when you are feeling it, and excuse me for sounding all hippy-ass spiritual glittery star cakes here, but when you have these positive vibes, others can sense them. The other day - true story - I walked seven miles listening to *Chicago V* and *Little Angels Young Gods* album. Everyone

I walked past nodded a greeting or said hi. I found it weird that everyone acknowledged me. But of course, they did. I was happy; I was grateful, and that can be felt by others. But to feel like that, takes the preparation and it can be easier just to feel a bit shit and ignore the world. In fact, most people do.

But you aren't 'most' people. But the world won't think your ace balls if you don't think you are. So, without sounding like a preacher, today's a great day to behave as the person you've always wanted to be.

And remember, change is like the movie *Armageddon* or *Rise of Skywalker*. Difficult at first, messy in the middle but awesome at the end.

We may laugh at Bon Jovi for his not amazing latest material, or his meaningless pop-fuelled tunes, but I don't. I think the world needs him for many reasons. One, he's cool, two he's got a hell of a pair of teeth and three, *Blaze of Glory* makes me wish I was on a horse shooting people which is a great thought. But mainly because he tells us not to be average. And if he was president, people would be like, "shit, yeah – let's not join the cult of average. Let's do it. I'll sleep when I'm dead, babe. I'll keep the faith, mediocrity is a crime, I'm going to be the best version of myself today, yeeee-aaaah. Now where's my cowboy hat?"

And how can that be a bad thing? Jon Bon Jovi is more Pooh than Eeyore. That sounded wrong, but you know what I mean. No matter how wise or mature I think I am, I can't help listening to his words of wisdom and thinking he's not done too badly for himself.

Being bad at something is easy. Being average at something is pretty easy too. So, most of us are just that. Then with hard graft, with reasons and motivation and inspiration, we become good at something. And good's okay. The weird thing is people stop there. But it's a smaller distance from good to great to awesome, than from bad to average to good. So, if you're getting good – then keep going. If you quit at good, you are like that dude who goes into the pub, spends all his money on the fruit machine, then bows out just before it pays out the jackpot to someone else who just put that last 50p in the machine because he was waiting for his girlfriend to come out of the loo.

I know I might sound like Jon himself, but goddammit, GO FOR GREAT.

And before you ask what greatness is, greatness is *not* what people think of you. Who cares? Well, in fact nearly everyone. But that's not the point. Stop trying to impress people. Impress yourself. Because if you can impress yourself then you better yourself. Pride is a wonderful thing.

Go out and be you. A lovely, kind, talented you that will inspire people. Then you have a purpose. And with that purpose, your passion will grow. And with that passion, you will become more motivated.

You will always get critics. That's life. People will knock you down, intentionally or not. Some people are just jealous, but most feel they need to give some guidance or advice so they feel validated. That's okay. But think of those that have gone before you.

Think of Freddie Mercury, Steven Tyler, Bonn Scott, Tommy Lee, Jimi Hendrix, Prince. Every one of these have been considered an oddball by someone.

Think of those whose paths you've treaded and ask yourself; did they care enough about what people said not to go with their creativity?

Let's be honest. Imagine if you were told about the concept of *Bohemian Rhapsody*. You probably would go, "erm..okay. How about just play a few verses, a bridge then a catchy chorus that goes nah-nah-nah?"

Dream big, start small and act now. And remember, the price of regret is always bigger than the price of discipline. If Jon Bon Jovi wants me to write his new album for him, I'm here. But seriously re-read that last sentence.

Another way you can help motivate yourself is reading. Yes - reading! An autobiography or biography should be placed down, your neurones should be pumping of impulses and you should get up and run to that guitar, bass, drum kit, notepad, microphone and get working. This doesn't have to be music related. Gandhi, and Nelson Mandela's biographies and Stephen King's book on writing were so inspiring, I just wanted to be a better person after every chapter. I read and re-read books written about one of my heroes, Andy Kaufman. I then put it down and ask myself, *how* he did what he did? What makes him different from me? Or different from anybody else. And the answer? The answer is usually the same – hard work, dedication and a belief in what they are doing. They are all inspired individuals. And as we have already established, you can help to motivate yourself to be, then inspire others.

So, go and lead, damn it. No matter who you are. You may be the singer, the frontman or frontwoman, the centrepiece of the band, the focal point. Or you may be more comfortable hiding behind a keyboard, a bass guitar or an unnecessarily large sized drum kit. It doesn't matter what you play or where you are situated. In your band, you lead. Freddie Mercury was the front man of Queen, his charisma and voice changed people's lives. Literally. John Deacon was quiet, just wanted to play his bass and get some of his songs played. Neither of them were less of a leader than the other. They were both leaders. They led. Leading isn't about showing off, being handsome, being loud or wearing tight trousers over a sock-filled cod piece. You can lead quietly or loudly, but you must lead. Remember, there are people in the future who may watch/listen to you and follow you, copy you. So, like it or not, you are a leader in your field.

Vaibhav Shah got in right when he said, "whenever you see a successful person you only see the public glories, never the private sacrifices to reach them."

I have numerous conversations with band members or students, telling me how it's not fair because other bands get the breaks and they don't. They tell me this band or that band got in this festival or that festival and they don't seem to be working very hard. If I had a pound for every time I was told that, I would be pretty damn rich. Maybe I'll ask for it. But and this might not surprise you - every band who say this to me aren't as good as the band they are talking about. When I say good, I mean it. And the reason the other band are hitting big things is simply because they are rehearsing, they are calculating the gigs, working hard on advertisements, working hard on supplying good EPKs or networking, whilst building up their brand with commitment and increasing their following day after day. This itself takes skill and hard work. If it was easy, everyone would do it. You only see the final product – remember that. For example, you are reading this book, you would be completely unaware of the fact I swore at my computer twice and the battle I had for spelling the word resilience. I've just doubled checked if that is spelt right again. It is.

So, go and change the future. Be that change.

Gandhi may have not loved Slipknot, but he knew what he was talking about when he said. “You must be the change you wish to see in the world.”

I had the chance to talk to three completely talented and inspiring female artists during the writing of this book and after conversations with all three, I got up and got busy. I had ants in my pants, and they taught me so much about music and life in general. We discussed what motivated them to spend their lives creating music - when in truth, life may be easier just doing a job and chilling out of an evening - watching soaps and re-runs of Vera. Last year, I read three powerful autobiographies which gradually changed my habits. Talking to Karly Jewell, Verity White and Imogen Rosemary had the same effect. Three talented, inspiring and amazing musicians.

Karly Jewell is an established Australian singer/songwriter. I began by asking her what got her started in the first place. Karly has had the baton passed by Tony Jewell, her grandfather. Tony Jewell wrote for many artists, including the biggest Australian country artist of all time - the late Slim Dusty. Karly describes her Grandad as, “not just a songwriter, also a poet and wonderful artist. He had also had a great involvement in starting country music festivals around the place.”

She says, “I started playing guitar the minute I could stand up and stand in front of him and try to play guitar. I got my first guitar when I was five years old. I think, just being around that lifestyle, always writing songs and music. He really inspired me and when he gave me a guitar – he gave it to me as a diary.”

A guitar as a dairy. That day, a couple hours after talking to Karly, I got thinking. A guitar as a diary? The thought really struck a chord. That’s what poetry is. Bob Dylan doesn't need to write a diary because he *is* a diary. I can look at the books I've read, and the books and stand-up comedy sets I've written, and I know where I was, who was in my life and how I was feeling. Keeping a diary doesn't have to be Adrian Mole-esk. It can be a body of work.

Karly talks about her Grandad, a huge influence in her life.

"He had a very hard life. As a police officer, he's seen a lot of horrible things and he used music as an escape and a place to go to. I've done the same thing; we don't wait for anything. I've put a lot of hard work in. People say, how do you do that? You must know someone."

She continues, "you've just got to keep at it and go for it. Some bands after eight years who don't get a label just give up. You don't wait for these things anymore; you just need to and create that on your own."

Even as a songwriter it's in the blood, there is nothing more you want to do than write songs. I was really inspired and with having that guitar as a diary to express yourself, you have that freedom to find yourself again and work your way through it."

The song writing process is obviously emotive and a huge part of Karly's art. And the bond it brings with her band and her fans is appreciated.

"There's the experience and that connection you have with people, some songs I cry when I sing. Someone else cries, then we all start crying. We build a really close music family around us. We do this together. There's that experience of travel and moments you just can't believe you are having from something you love so much."

I talked to Karly first thing in the morning due to the time difference between Melbourne and Stoke-On-Trent. I don't think a single day has been so productive once that call had finished. Talking to someone who regularly plays Melbourne and has graced the stage at the *Whiskey A Go-Go* with the same philosophy as you is pretty special.

"I never thought I'd play at the *Whiskey A-Go-Go* and stand where my idols stood. We were able to go to Vegas. It all came out of our pocket, but how amazing to be able to do that with music. Your band becomes your family. To be able to do that was amazing.

Karly's band have been travelling to the States for the last 8 years, and tour and building their profile in Los Angeles.

"When people say 'one Day, you'll make it' to me, I think - I already have made it because as long as I am doing something that I love, I don't care if I'm performing to a room of 500-600 people, or in an empty room to no one - I'm happy to play my guitar and write my songs."

I ask Karly about her song-writing. She mentioned that her bathroom was a great place the ideas came to her and how eventually, this experience was shared on social media.

"People want to see me being real, and I want to share that with people because without them, I would have no one to play to, they are the ones supporting us. A lot of people wanted to know where I write my songs, so I started doing some live videos from my bathroom, just me and my guitar.

People would say that's the girl from the bathroom. In a bathroom writing a song, I'm going to share that. Nothing fancy. Sometimes it'll get me when I'm cooking dinner. That's it, I can't cook dinner I've got this song in my head and I've got to work on it.

Sometimes I get a line and need to write it down. I was recently reading through some interviews my Grandad had. They used to ask him where he got his ideas and he would say - I had this idea and I would just write it down whenever."

Karly fascinated me with a story she told about her Grandad and how he wrote. She talked about finding a bit of timber in the shed with lyrics on it and then she had to go through all the garden, because he would write stuff down anywhere. "– it's like a treasure hunt. Don't throw that out, it may have lyrics on it. I have pieces of paper and tissue boxes and a piece of timber from the shed with lyrics on it."

"He taught me how to write songs. I wrote my first song when I was 16. The most important thing for you to know is, not everyone is going to like it, but other people will.

He told me, "never feel pressured to write for anybody else. It's *your* story and all that you can do is write and tell a story and the background will be music. That's what music is and that is the connection."

Writing is highly pressurised but to Karly it's not about pigeon-holing into a certain style.

"I don't write for anybody but me, and that opened up loads of doors as I only write with feeling. I have written heavy songs, which are played on rock radio and lighter songs on country radio stations. It gives me that freedom to write what I feel. I'm inspired by David Bowie and George Michael. I have always looked at those two because they did whatever they wanted. They would drift into anything. People say, 'just stick to what you know,' but for me it all depends on what I'm feeling. That's a freedom and such a great feeling to be able to do that.

It gave us a wider audience. We've got teenagers that listen and Dave's (bass player) uncle is a fan. He comes to the shows, he's early seventies. It's great, he loves all the songs. It's amazing to have that wide range."

Verity White should be a household name on Planet Earth. An artist who is the real deal. Her music is beautifully crafted and performed, and her high standards as a musician reflect her high standards as a human being. With two albums released and *After the Storm* released in 2020, together with her wonderful live appearances, Verity in an alternative universe where the world was fair, would be headlining Glastonbury. Verity knows the way of the music world and does everything for the right reasons. If you listen to her and see her and her band live, you will understand. Everything is given on stage. And every Verity White gig I have witnessed, the audience give it straight back.

"When I was little, I used to dance around restaurants, as you can imagine I loved being the centre of attention even then. My parents loved their music. They listened to Fleetwood Mac and Dire Straits. I remember listening to Blondie and Aretha Franklin and thinking, 'I want to sing.' Singing is awesome. Aretha Franklin really inspires me; she's a writer and she can sing with so much emotion. And I thought - wouldn't it be amazing if I could write music and sing and what I was singing could actually affect how other people felt. So, for me it was that emotional connection, that's what I want to do.

There's no better feeling in the world. We've had fans write us messages and come up to us after gigs and say, I'm so happy that you played that song because that brought me back from a bad place, or I'm really happy you played that because it really resonates with me.

And you actually change their lives. You've touched their lives. And to me, that's success.

It truly is the biggest compliment you can receive."

Verity passes that baton down the generations tightly and securely. How Verity listens to Aretha, there will be many people listening to Verity and modelling themselves on her. It's the circle of inspiration as clear as day. Verity White, clearly does not do this to be a megastar and earn billions of dollars, with her own reality television show and Kanye West popping in for milk. She does not do it for the ego check or the fame. And as I previously said, she is the real deal. I don't mean she is drinking *Jack Daniels* out of the bottle whilst rocking out in a foam party. The Verity White on stage and on record send the same message to the world. And it is an important one.

"I want to be known as someone who was written lyrics and sang songs that effect other people, impacted on how they feel and maybe even changed their opinion of things," she tells me. "As an outspoken female artist and someone who is open about mental health, I think it is really important to always be open and show openness and positivity.

Help people, discover themselves. As an artist, it's important to be relatable. I'm not someone who is egotistic and wants their own pedestal. I am just a normal human person who makes music and I hope people like it.

If you have fans, then your job is to make your fans happy. It is all about the fans and all about giving them a good time"

Again, catch Verity and her band live. Everybody is leaving the venue with a smile bigger than their faces.

Having chats with Verity and Karly were most excellent, so I decided to talk to Imogen Rosemary - the singer and songwriter from Novustory, a band who have been making large waves in the UK Rock scene. Again, Imogen is highly respected in the scene and I wondered where Novustory not only fitted in, but what got such a young, energic, emotive band where they is now. I asked Imogen who she had the baton from.

"To me", she said, "I was inspired by who your parents introduce you too – Nina Simone, Ella Fitzgerald and Etta James – seems a bit odd, but back then I was singing jazz."

I listen while thinking it doesn't sound odd at all. In fact, knowing how much emotion is mirrored in Novustory, it is now clear where that soulful side originated from.

"Then I listened to bands like Busted, stuff like that. Ella Fitzgerald and Busted", she says, laughing. Her laugh is contagious.

The Busted thing for me is massively interesting. I remember being in a pub in the centre of London and a tall guy came in with bright blond hair. A few people at the bar seemed to recognise him. I remember he was eating a *McDonalds*, and I thought it was a strange thing to do to bring a Maccie Dee's in a pub with you. It happened to be one of the dudes from the rock-pop-boyband Busted. My mate told me his feelings towards them. Let me tell you he wouldn't have got a gig at the Royal Variety Performance with the colourful language he displayed whilst talking about this band.

But to me, my opinion differed. I told him, without knowing their material but guessing what they sounded like, they must be a good thing because if it gets kids into rock music, then surely the next stage is that same kid liking more rock music, and eventually being a rock fan, maybe picking up an instrument and possibly forming a band. My friend at the time grunted something and we continued to talk about football, food and people we remembered from school.

But now, twenty years later I am pleased to say I was correct. Imogen was that person and that pleases me. I called my friend in question to give him the told-you-so comment and we continued our conversation about people from school.

Anyhow, back to Imogen and her journey from then to here.

"I started hanging around with people, went through *the High School Musical* phase and *Hannah Montana* phase, not yet finding my identity in music. I get a lot of inspiration from Young Blood. Young Blood - he's gone and taken the rule book and decided not to use it. Wear what you want, be you are. A punk approach. I love Dream State, we supported them and fell in love. I love the punk attitude. Don't box yourself in."

I talk to Imogen about legacies. What is it she wants to be remembered for? Her smile widens "I want people to talk about us how I just talked about Young Blood, you can be 100 percent yourself," she says. "I want to make people to be themselves, and they can let go.

I write the lyrics. I write about personal experience, about abusive relationships or eating disorders and I make it relatable to people who have suffered the same kind of things, or similar. Many people comment – your lyrics speak to me, I feel understood.

We help people through different emotions – that's what I want our legacy to be."

Image is important, but always hold true to yourself. It takes some people a lifetime to learn this lesson. Imogen has clocked it early in life and her wisdom shows.

"I was desperately trying to be something I wasn't. I always had fake tan and eyelashes on and was always wearing dresses because I felt I needed to look pretty, then I was really uncomfortable. My dress was a bit tight and I couldn't sing properly, my skirts too small so I can't dance."

Now I go on stage in what I feel comfortable in on the night, we did a show at the *Bread Shed* in Manchester, I wasn't worried about ticket sales because we had done really well, I wasn't worried about my voice because I had looked after it. I was actually worried about what I was going to wear. Literally something switched in my head, I thought fuck this, people are here to hear me sing not to judge my outfit. I wore ripped leggings and a baggy 5XL jumper.

Everyone was saying, this is the most connected we have felt with you, the most you've jumped around. From that moment on, I felt I don't have to wear makeup or wear a dress for anyone. It took me a long-time to get that. I needed to get that out of my head. They aren't bothered. They are there to see the band performing songs they like.

When you are going on *X Factor?* they ask me. 'Never', I say." Her smile widens again.

"People are connecting with lyrics and songs."

And that is why Imogen and Novustory are a success story. Yes, their music kicks more ass than Bruce Lee in a pinata factory, but their philosophy is great. Many bands pay good money for this advice. Novustory have cracked the code with their ace attitude towards their own art.

You can't feel it if you can't feel it, right? I mean, when you feel like a sack of crap, eating healthy as if you were on a weight loss mission or doing your twenty-minute hit-class or picking up that *Fender* is difficult, right? Of course it is, you feel like crap. That sinking feeling is pulling you down and you are being smothered with the cant-be-arsed blanket. The same blanket that drops your shoulders, pulls at your eyelids and tells you to forget about the whole thing. This is natural. But unfortunately, cyclic. You can't be bothered to be productive, so you eat a whole tub of salt and vinegar *Pringles* and watch the *Channel 5* movie. You don't want to, but you do. Then you feel guilty because 1) you didn't have it on your list 2) You were calorie counting 3) You had a million things to do, including writing that song, reading that book or you promised to call someone 4) the film was a bit shit and you never really watched it – you just scrolled on your phone.

Then because you feel guilty you think, bugger this – today's a write off, let's start again tomorrow.

This isn't depression, anxiety or sadness. This, my friends is human nature. If you didn't have days like this – well, I would be jealous. I don't have an answer, but I can tell you what I do to get myself in the mood. To snap out of it as they say. I use the practice of anchoring. Yes, anchoring. I don't know if that's the technical term, but it works. Well, works for me, so give it a go.

You see; mood is emotion and we can control these emotions. So can others. Others manipulate our feelings constantly. Advertisements don't sell products, they sell emotions. We fundamentally know this. I actually cry at some adverts. I hate some of them I love some of them. What do they sell? Who knows? Sometimes I love an advert so much I hope it comes on. You know the one? Great jingle, man with a funny accent and a cool hat? Not the one with the talking frog or the dancing cat, the other one. I tell people I love this advert. "Which one?" They ask. "You know the one," I say and explain it. Eventually the conversation goes like this.

"See that advert. Man, I love it."

"Which one?"

"The one that goes ta-ta-ta at the end and it's got that funny dude on the sofa."

"Hmmm, don't think I've seen it."

"You must have. It's got that talking dog. Digital trickery obviously, but man, it's funny."

"What's it advertising?"

"Dunno. Insurance maybe? Dog food? Sofas? Don't know, really. But I *love* it."

Because they sell emotions. Like movies do. How much do I love the movie Armageddon? The answer, loads. It's amazing. I cry every time. Is it because Bruce has saved the whole world from an asteroid? Is it that his daughter and the handsome bloke who played Batman can now marry? Is it for the crazy dude who gets jiggy with the prostitute Molly Mount, on the runway? Possibly. But my tears fall, because as these incidences occur they blast on some chuuunage which manipulates my emotions. Steven sings, "don't want to miss a thing," and by golly my eyes flow more salty tears than they do at the end of an episode of DIY SOS, or when Mickey dies in Rocky III (sorry for the spoiler if you haven't seen it). Emotions are powerful and that's why they use them for us to buy their products.

Meerkats – say no more.

The trick is to alter these emotions of yours. Easy? No. Possible, yes. Certain sounds and smells will make you happy. We know this. Bizarrely, the sound of crockery makes me a little happy – it takes me back to my childhood holidays in Bonskeid House in Pitlochry, which I used to attend and love. The sound of snooker balls colliding, I find soothing. The smell of rubber reminds me of buying my first skateboard in a shop in Broughty Ferry and being served by a woman called Megan. I have no idea what she looked like or who she really was, but I remember the smell. The rubber smell came from the bike tires and not Megan, I'll add here. (The very same skateboard has since been signed by Alice Cooper and is still in my possession if anyone ever wants to see it.)

Eighties classics stir something in me. Not particularly because I'm a fan, but they bring me back to a time and a place; a time of youth when you didn't worry about bills, weight, the world's injustice or if your battery on your phone will hold out. Whitney *Houston's I Wanna Dance With Somebody*, Dead or Alive's *You Spin me Round*, and Baltimora's *Tarzan Boy* probably aren't classics. But you know what? They make me happy. They bring a smile to my face and my mood has switched. They have *anchored* me for a fleeting moment in a particular time and place. It doesn't matter that it was a fleeting visit, as my mood has now changed. My neural pathway has diverted into a better route. It's that simple.

My anchors are a strange breed. Fundamentally and musically I understand Chicago 16 isn't as good as Chicago Transit Authority. But Chicago 16 is an anchor for me. It has the ability to change the direction of my neural pathways. There are others. Huey Lewis and the News, Hootie and the Blowfish, Bon Jovi's *Slippery When Wet*, Iron Maiden's *Seventh Son of a Seventh Son*, *Young Gods* by Little Angels, *Stranger in This Town* by Richie Sambora, Queen's *The Miracle*. The list goes on.

My advice is to find your anchors, get them on a playlist and the next time your mood dips, get on it. You can catch it before you start sinking. Because once you start sinking, you choose not to use them. You succumb to the feeling of emptiness. Go on do it now. Put a bookmark in the page and find your anchors. The title of your playlist can be called anything. I have around 20 playlists and uncreatively called Playlist 1-20. These can be shared or kept private – whatever you want.

Another anchor of mine is soundtracks. I don't know how good the *Top Gun* or *Lost Boys* soundtrack actually is, but they anchor me to a time and a place and by God, they work. When I hear *Playing With The Boys* or *People Are Strange*, my negative thoughts leave my mind quicker than Prince Andrew in a nightclub full of reporters.

Go find your anchor and don't feel bad about it. Sometimes we feel we *should* feel bad, so we do. But feeling rotten isn't helping anyone. Go find your song and plug yourself in. Personally, with the combination of cutlery clattering, a cup of tea and *Hip To be Square* playing, I am in a good place. My anchors have hooked me down and I'm feeling good. Yes, I realise that sounds like a Hot Chocolate lyric.

Every time I listen to *Just Push Play* by Aerosmith, my memory takes me back to Melbourne, Australia. I was backpacking and noticed that the Hard Rock Café was playing the whole album before it was released. I sat at the bar on my own, buying overpriced beer and listened to the whole thing. It may not be the best Aerosmith album ever, but to me it's beautiful. I don't remember anything else of that day, but when *Fly Away From Here* comes on, I smile and taste that cold beer. Magical.

The beauty with anchors is, we can make them. I know, huh! Here's what you do. I know you may feel a bit silly doing this. But that's okay. I spend my time standing next to a microphone-stand trying to make people laugh. Silly is okay. But this will be worth it. Find a physical movement, one that makes you happy. Be it a fist pump, some floss dancing, a massive whoop of laughter, a huge shit-eating grin. Find your physical movement.

Got it? Great. Now do it. Go on. If you can't because you keep on laughing brilliant. Now, do it five, six, seven times. Repeat it and smile. Feels good, right? And now you've made your anchor. The next time your inner workings decide to take your thoughts in the wrong direction, do that movement. If it was your floss-dance then you are excused from performing it in *Kwik-Fit.* It could be something subtle, a stroke of the earlobe, a rub of the neck, a click of the fingers. It's going to be your new anchor. Anchors work as they change your thought pattern. Go on, clench your fist and shout, "yes!" Feels good, see?

Be aware of your inner emotions and keep a hold of these good vibrations.

Years ago, I felt miserable and I was strongly persuaded I needed to go to the doctor for pills. There was a part of me that felt it wasn't the answer. Before anyone thinks I'm saying pills don't work, I'm not. This was *my* experience. Depression can be paralysing, and I don't believe I was depressed. I was unhappy. Yes. Very unhappy. Miserable. I asked myself the question on the bus, what I would like to change about me. The answer was everything. I narrowed it down. And made a decision to change one thing at a time.

It was a rough ride. Months of months of pain, of sadness, of guilt. I didn't want to listen to my favourite *Hootie and the Blowfish* album because I felt guilty. I had hurt people and wasn't the best version of me that I was capable of.

But eventually I got there. I read autobiographies. I listened to music. I smiled and laughed. There is nothing in my current situation that I would change. Well, I would love to have hair. Cool hair like Slash or that cool guy from that dance act that I occasionally see. He's always smiling, and I like him.

Knowing what exactly you want is not easy. Happiness is not an answer, because that is a feeling. Money, fame, fortune, fast cars and designer watches may make you happy. But they might not? Ask *why you* want these things. Because if it's to make yourself happy, you can do that without a jewel-laced codpiece made from Emu skin. I watch these television shows sometimes about these posh hotels and their residents. They don't seem over the moon to me. In fact, I reckon you see more smiles at a local gig that at *The Ritz.*

I ask myself, very regularly if I had a lamp and had three wishes what would they be? Then once I know my wishes instead of wishing for them, I attempt to make them happen. Then as if by magic, once I have written down (with a pen – remember the physical aspect I talked about) some simple steps to get what I want, I feel better. It's all about taking control. And knowing your mind. Two things that sound easier than they are.

Many many years ago now, in fact the summer of 1992. I was 19 years old, and I was at *Donington Monsters of Rock* festival. It was going to be a long day, but the opening act blew me away. *The Almighty* stood on that stage and played a set that could be from a Hollywood movie. I watched as the ginger lead singer growled into the microphone from start to finish, singing songs from their debut album. The performance was perfect; the musicianship was spot-on and the chat in between some of the songs was inspiring. I still remember the opening song *Crucify*, to the closing *Free n Easy* and *Wild and Wonderful.* What a show! What a performance. Timeless. So, imagine my joy when 28 years later I caught up with this singer, who is also the frontman of Thin Lizzy and Black Star Riders. His solo material is sensational also.

I asked Ricky Warwick, who was his biggest inspiration in this world.

"My biggest inspiration is my father, a genuinely great man. Always looked up to and always respected. He was always very supportive about what I did."

Ricky told me a story about when he played football when he was younger and scored a hat-trick for the team. He told me his Dad watched the game and he turned to him in the car on the way home and said, "show off." Not well done but show off.

"My Dad knew you were always as good as your last game. You're only as good as the last song you write, you're only as good as your last show and that work ethic. He showed me you had to work hard for everything. That was instilled in me. Nothing is free, you work hard to get it and you'll get it. That installed the work ethics in me."

"Seeing all the glam bands Slade, Sweet, *T-Rex* and being mesmerised by how they looked and the sounds they made, and I was hooked and then punk came along. Thin Lizzy came along, Stiff Little Fingers came along. And with them being Irish and I thought these guys are from the island I'm from, they can do it. How do I unlock that door? How do I join that room and get into that meeting with those great bands? I found it fascinating."

Ricky is just as enthusiastic and fascinating off stage than on stage. He continues talking about who influenced him with gusto and passion. "And still to this day if it wasn't for Phil, or for Jake Burns. Phil from Lizzy, Jake from Still Little Fingers. They were the *driving force*. I want to be part of that. I have to be part of that all costs, I thought."

I'm an only son and my dad being a farmer, my life was mapped out for me. Coming home at 16 to work on the farm. That's what was going to happen and that's what I did. That's exactly what I did, and music got in the way. My dad realised my passion about music and realised that was my calling. I felt about music what my father felt about farming. It was in his blood, up 5.30 in the morning and done at 10 at night. I felt the same for music, and my dad was smart enough to see that. Instead of dissuading me, he encouraged me. Which is a mark of a great man. He said, go for it.

That was the inspiration."

For me, Ricky Warwick is one of my heroes. A man who oozes talent and works his rock n roll socks on. For all my adult life, I've been listening to his music and catching his band live. I Ask him what he wants his legacy to be. What is important to leave behind?

"I would like to think people know I'm straight up, I call it how it is, I would like to think I have a good legacy of work. I'm still creating, I'll create and write songs right up until I pass away because I love it so much. I think it's leaving a good, honest and solid legacy of work – and being remembered for being a good person and entertaining people and putting a smile on people's faces. Being a good person, being a great husband and father is probably the most important thing.

I've no aspirations to do anything else, I live for it; I love it; it makes me who I am. Loved it since I was 14 years old. I'm doing it because I love it.

I'm been doing it long enough that I kinda know what I'm doing," he tells me. This could be the understatement of the decade. If Politics was a game of rock-and-roll, Ricky Warwick would be President and the best, most trusted, reliable, innovative damn president the world has ever seen.

"Seeing the look on people's faces, seeing them singing along, that big smile, seeing that fist in the air. Knowing you have connected them. There's that connection there. Job done. I've made a difference. The buzz is phenomenal. There's nothing better. You thrive of it. There's nothing better. It empowers you and makes you want to do better and put on a great show.

It's entertainment, you are there to entertain these people. They can forget about anything and focus on the music. It's the same for us. When we are playing, we are forgetting about all that shit at home and we are just playing music.

I wanted to be Phil Lynott, Lemmy, Jake Burns - these guys were fucking cool. So, if I can inspire someone, change the way they think, inspire them from one of my songs, I think it is great. Because that's what happened to me. I'm just passing it on."

The baton passing is well and truly visible here and hearing about it floods you with inspiration. Ricky also speaks about what is important in a band. Song writing. And the importance of producing a good song. One of Ricky's lyrics asks, "are you Keith Richards in reverse?" Brilliant! But as Ricky knows, some of these newer bands do it all – apart from the bread and butter. Delivering the songs.

He talks about these bands. "We'll get wasted," he says, "we'll go on Facebook and brag about it, but where's the *fucking* songs?

I loved The Almighty we had the swagger and the attitude, but we *also* had the songs. The Mohammed Ali syndrome. He could talk the talk, but boy he could *walk* the walk as well.

I'm working with a couple of young bands I keep on telling them – it's the songs that count"

And Ricky knows best. Personally, if you were in a band and Mr Warwick was giving you advice – take it and grab it with both hands. It will be priceless.

I also had the opportunity to catch up with Emma Hodgson, the singer from a newer band on the scene, False Hearts. I've had the privilege to introduce False Hearts to the stage three or four times over the past year or so and every time they bring it home. Great tunes and a fantastic live band, so catching up with Emma was hugely interesting.

I asked her who she grabbed the baton from and who she plans to pass it to.

"When I was growing up, my Dad was into his rock (Rolling Stones, Queen, Clapton, Beatles - and mum was more into her Motown and Abba and melodic stuff.

I watched my local heroes in the community playing, and I thought to myself, I would like to do that. But I thought I wouldn't and said to myself that I never would.

What's going on, I thought. Everybody is doing what they love, why don't I just do it?

I am so proud of myself and I am so glad I pushed myself to do it. People around me are responsible for pushing me in the right direction. People assume you are a born showman or born to do this, but sometimes you're not. It's very hard. But people were patient and supportive."

It's amazing speaking to Emma because she's the proof that you don't have to be an attention seeking ego-fuelled narcissist to be on stage. Although a wonderful frontwoman and incredible on stage, Emma is exceptionally modest and has a quiet demeanour.

"Being someone who is shy and quiet, sensitive, nervous and emotional and told you could never to do it and then realising I can do it and I'm going to give it a good try. And just enjoy the journey. It's not about making it and having to be big - it's about doing it. The first gig we did was at a gig in Cambridge, we never thought we would get there. That was the big highlight. Everything higher than that is making it."

We talk further about inspiration and the feeling she gets from inspiring others.

"Inspiration is everything," she says. "Especially the younger generation, younger girls look up and say they want to do that themselves. It feels incredible. To be an inspiration feels mad. You have that responsibility to show people the positive.

It's not about image, how you present yourself etc, it is about the music. That's it. Simple."

It's fascinating talking to Emma. Somebody who is on the journey and thoroughly enjoying every step. I ask what advice she would give someone else who possibly hasn't taken that first step yet and maybe is anxious about what is to be expected from them.

"Why are you trying to be someone else? I would ask. Just be you. Stop trying to be someone else. Do it as yourself."

Emma informed me, this was advice she got from Joe, whose band Hollowstar are insanely wonderful. It's great advice. And Emma and False Hearts are truly inspiration, and demonstrate *why* you should go and just have fun, work hard and create brilliant art.

CHAPTER 4: DISTRACTIONS AND TASKS

Your life is way too important to give in to distractions. And distractions are the enemy. Green Day once told us to *Know Your Enemy*. You too, it's distraction, pal. I thought of a movie. It's about a superhero who is out there to be the best damn superhero he can be. In doing so he requires self-discipline, his ninja monk dude friend, who was the wisest man he knew, taught him that. This superhero went to the gym, helped everyone he could, played bass guitar like a bad-ass and spent all his spare time helping the local dog hospice. But like all superhero movies, there is a bad guy. This supervillain was called, Dr Distraction and he did heinous things, like give our hero unlimited data on his phone so he could scroll the net looking at memes, and got him entangled in an argument about something he really didn't give a shit about, but there was someone online who was being a right dick and our hero needed to prove him wrong.

Your life is way too important to be ruled by distraction.

Remember Groundhog Day. It sucked, right? No, not the film that was awesome but the idea of being stuck in a loop repeating the same day in and out, in and out.

But that's what happens to us.

I'm going to use myself as an example here, but I'm pretty sure this is a regular problem. And one that can be fixed. Let's look at *Facebook. Facebook* is great. You can connect, you can laugh at your friends' photos, advertise your products, advertise your gigs, see a cat float around a kitchen floor on a homemade ship made of cardboard and tonka truck wheels.

However, this is the kicker. Focus is the key to creation. Focus gives you the power to inspire others with your art. In fact, it's the key.

"How you do anything is how you do everything."

One of the most important quotes in this book. How many times have I written, taught, exercised, read, wrote with one eye on my task and the other somewhere else? Too many. You see if your attention is spread then that's exactly what it is. Instead of giving 100% to your job at hand, whether writing a song, improving something, drawing, writing, reading - you might give 60%. My work deserves 100% of my time. For the reason my work may inspire someone in the future and *they* deserve 100% effort.

Imagine if Steven Tyler kept on leaving the stage to watch the football results? I once saw a huge rock band at Wembley and the singer checked his watch. I caught it but gave him the benefit of the doubt. But then he checked it again. For the rest of the gig, I felt he really didn't deserve my £60. I felt cheated. We must focus.

You know when you are on the phone and someone is not paying attention. You can hear it in their absence. It's frustrating, right? How many times have you just wanted to pick up a phone from someone's hand and smash it against the wall and scream, "listen to me!" like a five-year-old kid. It happens. So, let's get focused.

I find the word resilience is over-used, but I can see why. The kids I work with usually look at something which seems impossible and says, "I can't do it." Usually with a plethora of quite impressive excuses. When you say, "think about it," they don't. You can't force someone to think. You can nudge them, try to persuade them, even sigh and shake your head, but you cannot force them. It's an art form to sit down, to think about the problem or task. And in order to do it, distraction needs to get out of your life quicker than Katie Hopkins.

So, back to *Facebook*. Think about this. How many times do we check social media for no apparent reason? I look to see how many tickets I've sold for a show then the next thing I know, forty minutes have passed and I've scrolled past many a meme of how shit 2020 is and know exactly how many people laughed at my Prince Andrew joke. Then wait until it gets one more shocked or laughing emoji.

It's funny, right? I think I'm a busy bee. I am. I like being busy. But am I just busy being busy some of the time? I would say no, absolutely not. Look what I've done today? But actually, *Facebook* tells me differently. Two and a half hours on this social media platform. And let's be honest, ten minutes posting a radio advert, ten minutes tagging people, then the remaining two hours and ten minutes checking replies, checking for likes and seeing if Arleen's ex-boyfriend has responded to the bitchy message by her sister.

I understand there is a shot of dopamine produced every time your post gets a reaction, a like, a love, a smiley face, a weird yellow thing holding a red thing. But that's short-term. Remember, the price of discipline is always greater than the pain of regret. Your focus will give you a bigger and better dopamine kick when you produce something which is star-spangled awesome and your sense of pride kicks in. Feeling pride is an immense feeling which sticks on you and builds your foundations and your worth. The shot of dopamine is like eating a Big Mac.

It's pretty nice but doesn't last long, then makes you feel a bit empty.

Our addiction to social media comes from our innate disposition to gossip. We love it. Hence Emmerdale, Coronation Street and EastEnders. Our ancestors may have needed information to calculate areas to scavenge and hunt without being attacked, or to form relationships with the right people. Unfortunately, we have evolved, became taller, less hairy, and have developed the art of writing and drawing to exchange valuable information. Yet our requirement to gossip has remained.

We get hooked in to gossiping, and ultimately it effects our positive vibrations. Does EastEnders make anybody happy? At best it scatters your attention. Your focus won't be complete as some of that attention and focus will be lost on you thinking about Geoff and why he really shouldn't have had that affair with Steve, because their respective wives know each other and are in fact sisters.

Our mind is like a chimp doing gangham style as it is. Our neurones are firing in all directions and gossiping and flicking through *Facebook* isn't helping. In fact, and I don't believe this is just me – sometimes I am so angry at what I read on social media – I go on further visits to *Twitter* and *Facebook* and look for things I don't want to read, so I can comment on them. Yes, I do. Then all I need to do is keep my phone permanently in my hand and regularly check these idiot's responses. Yeah, I'll teach these keyboard warriors a lesson or two. But I'll get less work done as I'm not focused. And ultimately damage my own creativity.

And the thing with keyboard warriors is they *want* a response. Why else would they write a post on how angry they are at the government's policy or the global climate crisis? So ask yourself the question – do you want to focus on a job to do, grab that song, master that solo, develop a killer riff that may be played in every pub covers band from here until the end of the century, or question why someone doesn't like Greta Thunberg.

My advice: Stay clear of drama and focus on your talent.

As Jane Austen said in Pride and Prejudice, "keep your breath to cool your porridge." And she knew what she was talking about. And she loved Metallica.

Break these hooks and get focused. Focus your attention on one thing and make it an important thing. This includes everything. Playing, talking to someone, reading this book. (If your phone is at hand, drop it. Drop it now, before you check to see if she's read your WhatsApp message by the display of the green ticks.)

Robbie Williams does it well. I watched a couple minutes of his Live at Knebworth show on the telly. What he does, he does well. One thing I noticed as he winks at a member of the audience. There's 70,000 people there. And around 30,000 people thought he was winking at them. It doesn't matter. He made people feel special by focusing on them.

I'm not saying you must work all the time, 24/7. Of course not. Your mind is a ball of complex material which needs time to rest and develop, just like a muscle. But procrastinating isn't resting because you just feel a bit crap while doing it and your mind is still making excuses about not doing things.

Like good sleep, your mind needs to disconnect for a while. Disconnect from social media. It's tough. I find myself before a gig on the socials, always. After the gig, I make a decision to put down my phone and not check it. But my hand doesn't seem to want to part with it. It feels exposed, naked. Before I know it, my phone is in my hand and I'm flicking through my socials quicker than my mate Dave flicks on *Tinder*.

There are many things you can do to disconnect and re-adjust these neurons. Many people meditate. I for one find it difficult. My thoughts go from soothing clouds to thinking of jokes, humming Slave to The Grind by Skid Row and deciding on what I want for a tea and justifying a take-away.

I discovered what I do is a practice called active mindfulness. I don't call it this; I call it – just switching off and chilling out. I do this with one of the best weapons in my armoury. The jigsaw. The jigsaw, you ask. Surely, you can't be serious. I am serious and don't.... anyway, yes – the jigsaw. I buy a 1000-2000-piece jigsaw of the coolest thing I can. Be it Star Wars, KISS album covers, dogs playing poker and smoking cigarettes. I have a jigsaw mat I keep under the sofa, for two reasons. One, it's out of the way and two, if I have visitors, I don't resemble a granny. I spend maybe three-four hours a week on it. Possibly half an hour an hour before I go to sleep. The physical feelings of the wooden parts, the idea that it might slow down dementia. I don't know what it is, but it works. It's like a drug. Be it the most boring uncool drug in the history of the world, but a drug it is like. Your phone must be away. Sometimes I listen to an album or the radio. However, within five minutes I have no sensation of it. Active mindfulness, zoning out, going with the flow, disconnecting, sitting in your pants putting together blocks of pretty pictures – whatever you call it. For me, it works.

Here are a couple easy tasks for you.

- Try a jigsaw or a puzzle of some kind – away from your phone.
- Go onto *Facebook*. On your Settings and Privacy, there is a Time on *Facebook* link. Go on it and attempt to lessen this daily.
-

Towards the end of 2018 I supported a band who I had fallen in love with many years before. Marc and Slyder, together with Tim Emery and Rik Pratt form the Last

Great Dreamers. Their debut album is now celebrating 25 years and LGD are probably one of the best kept secrets in UK rock. After taking nearly two decades off, the band reformed and released three brilliant albums to high acclaim in 2014, 2016 and 2018. The bands resurgence is due to hard work and constant touring, which they've honed into an immense live performance shimmering with glam powerpop rock.

It was ace to catch up with Marc Valentine and Slyder Smith to talk about inspiration, motivation and all things music. Slyder and Marc told me about where they first picked up the baton from.

"I went to my first gig when I was 11 and immediately knew I wanted to be on stage doing what they were doing" Slyder tells me.

Marc: "The very first band I remember seeing on TV were the Sweet - probably when I was about five. Their hooks and humorous flamboyance really stood out to me and left a huge impression as my first introduction to rock music. It probably sowed the seeds for my musical career...that, and of course my dad playing his guitar along to Buddy Holly records on a Sunday afternoon. He had the only electric guitar on our street which held a certain mystique and reverence back in those days. It was a red Watkins Rapier and always came out at family parties!"

Slyder adds "yes, it was very similar for me - watching TV and being glued to the screen when Top of The Tops was on...I think access to music was very limited then, not like now. When I was very young, probably under five I can remember watching Alvin Stardust, Mud and Suzi Quattro"

Marc: "Oooh Suzi Quattro yes I loved her too. I remember her performances so vividly.. it blew my mind as a kid!"

Slyder : "I also have a very early memory of my parents playing Gilbert O'Sullivan records at night when I was in bed. At the time music was always on - everywhere in the house"

Marc, Slyder and I continue to shoot the breeze, as we did up and down the M1 and many a late night in a Holiday Inn (and numerous Travelodge's). Slyder says "I recall when we got back together, it was very exciting. I mean, it had been 17 years since we were last together! It was emotional. I remember feeling the anticipation of that we were actually going to be doing this again, after all that time away. It was incredible the moment we stepped back onstage....maybe you could say a little rough around the edges to begin with, but such a great feeling to be back together again"

"Somehow this time around it means so much more to us. The appreciation of the fans and their devotion to following us up and down the country, their continued support and the journey they are taking with us. " Marc chips in "I couldn't agree more. The original fans and all the new fans and friends that we've made along the way are what makes this all worthwhile. After such a long hiatus we didn't know what to expect. We had gone our separate ways for several years and at first it felt kind of weird that we might actually resurrect the Dreamers - because when we split in the late 90's it really did feel like the dream was over. We were approaching our 30's and our second major record deal had just fallen through. At the time we thought it was too late and we were past it. Little did we know!."

"But you have to understand that back in those days the music industry discarded you pretty quickly if your first album didn't sell as well as they wanted. Bands weren't given much time to develop. At the time British music was constantly changing and evolving and sometimes it just chewed you up and spat you out. So, yes like Slyder says, I think that this time round for us it has been so different. It felt almost like a second bite at the cherry, yet we already knew the pitfalls and we've been through both the good and bad times. I guess it felt like we'd already done our apprenticeship and training. Although you never really stop learning and there's always a new challenge. Anyway, this time we decided to do it just for ourselves and the fans - and enjoy it simply for the music...the real reason why we're here. Try not to get too snagged up in the business and bullshit again, as you can end up losing sight of what's actually right in front of you. We take nothing for granted though, and we know how fragile it all is. After all these years we still get that unique rush of excitement when writing new songs and the immense thrill of performing, just the same as we ever have - in fact it never diminishes. Somehow it seems more special now - whether we're playing in front of 20 people or 2000, the buzz is still there"

Slyder tells me "Yes, I think we definitely appreciate it all so much more now. I hope that our legacy will be that we wrote and produced good songs that were from the heart. Whilst being well dressed! So ultimately I guess we'd like to think we did it our way, despite how hard the road was sometimes."

Mark smiles "haha you could say the clothes are almost as important as the music!"

Slyder expands " I think both our influences come from that glam rock period and when we first started we were part of the sleaze rock scene in London. It was an exciting time and a great place to be. The way you dressed was such a big part of it" Marc smiles at the memory "those influences made us who we are now and yeah I think we always tried to be authentic and completely immersed in what was going on"

Slyder continues "when our first album came out, me and Marc were in Sainsbury's buying our beer and pot noodles - dressed up to the nines in our flares and velvet jackets, then back to my flat in my 70's Ford Cortina. We weren't on our way to our gig, we were just living it, that was our lives" I ask them how it feels to pass on this ever-continuing baton of musical inspiration. How does it feel that future generations could be inspired Last Great Dreamers? Slyder says "It's a huge compliment and hopefully a lasting testament to our music. I've even seen ads for musicians looking to start bands, where their influences include Last Great Dreamers. It really means a lot" Marc "yes, just knowing that a song we've written plays a part in someone's life is very humbling. Whether it's one of our albums being blasted in the car on the way to work in Grimsby, or on someone's headphones in a factory in Frankfurt, it's just amazing and very life affirming. I think I'm beginning to realise just how lucky we are to be creating music, however small it might be in the grand scheme of things" I finish our conversation, asking for any advice for new bands out there.

Slyder smiles "I remember some advice that Marc gave me back at our first gig in 1989, just as we were about to go onstage...."lads, don't forget to jump around a lot!' " Marc "haha that's right! what a nugget of wisdom that was!" Marc continues "I think for any bands starting out right now, I would say just take your

> time to find your own sound and always be true to yourselves. Don't worry about what other bands are doing, just concentrate on writing good songs and develop your craft. Always be grateful and appreciative of everyone you meet along the way and keep your ego in check. Give it your blood, sweat and tears... and make sure every gig feels like it's the last night on earth" It is always a pleasure catching up with Marc and Slyder. They are incredible, talented people who never fail to put on one hell of a show.

It was always a pleasure catching up with Marc and Slyder. They are incredible, talented people who never fail to put on one hell of a show. Another guy who owns the stage just as much as Robert DeNiro owns the character, is one of the best bass players in the UK today. This dude is a powerhouse and his energy levels reach skyscraper levels. I caught up with Mr Berty Burton, the Angus Young of the Bass world. Berty plays in the brilliant Tigertailz and has also played with The Last Great Dreamers, Beth Blade and the Beautiful Disasters and is now a member of The City Kids. The man is everywhere and wherever he is, it's a great place.

I ask him about how he caught the rock n roll bug and who from. What makes Berty be Berty?

"I wasn't inspired by bass players but was inspired solely by bands. My biggest inspiration and still favourite band to this day is AC/DC. I grew up and religiously watched AC/DC videos, live DVDs, I remember getting the *Stiff Upper Lip* Live DVD and getting the albums and literally paved the way for me. Took me down the line.

Angus Young isn't the singer, but the focal front of that band. Like Slash, so I loved watching the DVDs, watching Angus running around, this complete character, this non-static creature running all over the stage and it stuck with me. Obviously, I love the music but watching him was amazing. I was transfixed by learning what they were all about."

Berty's enthusiasm cranks up a gear and you can sense the gift of wonder; music has given him.

"That taught me how to play music, it's such an easy band to play, as in playing along to it – it's an aint broke don't fix it mentality which I love."

We talk about music further and how, as a fan being on that stage and playing is an honour and a privilege. Our conversation goes to Metallica's second bassist, Jason Newsted.

"He was a fan of the band as well as being in the band," Berty tells me. "He was full on enjoying the band; he looks like he's having fun and that shows on your playing."

If you've ever had the pleasure to see Mr Burton on the stage, you can see the dude is enjoying himself more than my friend's hyperactive kid In Whacko's - the soft play zone.

"Say to people they should come up and say hello and I ask, 'Did you enjoy the show?' You know what? I hope they did but if they didn't, I couldn't care less because I enjoyed myself.

The one thing that humbled me was when I did a show ten years ago, way before Tigertailz, I was playing bass for New Generation Superstars, we played a show in London, there were a few people there. The guy who supported us was great and he was also a bass player and he says, 'you are my favourite bass player at the moment, I love doing what you do on stage.' That meant a lot. Due to that I fixated on playing my bass behind my head.

I love the showmanship. I watched music DVD's such as Iron Maiden, Black Label Society and learned from them. I did it so often the New Generation Superstars boss said to me at the time 'You didn't play your bass behind your head last night'. Of course, crowd turnouts help to show off, like at the HRH Sleaze festival standing in front of three thousand people you are going to be pumped and showcase yourself.

Sometimes I bash the back of my head when I swung it around," he laughs. "Yes, a bit showy sometimes, but then knowing the right time to do it is important. For example, in Tigertailz, it suits it and they have the reputation and it fits. With the 80s glam style of music, it works very well.

The first proper thing I invested in was a wireless set up so I could run around, I walked into the crowd, around the venues, in Germany I sprained my ankle – slept with my *converse* on my foot because it wouldn't come off - but the audience loved it and more importantly, I loved it and it got a reaction. People might go fucking yaaay or think you are a tosser, a right strutting peacock but it gets a reaction and that's what matters."

Berty's philosophy of enjoyment and showmanship is contagious. Personally, I found that lack of stagecraft missing in the nineties with the Cool Britannia vibe. It's great to speak to Berty. It reminds you that energy and fun are not only allowed but are to be applauded.

We talk about his legacy. In fifty years' time how would the world remember the powerhouse flamboyant bass player Berty Burton.

"I would love to be remembered as a solid rock n roll bass player. People know me as a bass player, playing the Thunderbird bass. For me personally, known as a rock n roll bass player like Gene Simmons, Lemmy or Duff McKagen. The biggest Rock n roll bands on the planet and these guys are holding down the foundations."

I ask if Mr Burton has any advice, he would part to anybody in a band, kicking of their career and beginning to carve the path that their heroes have followed. To Berty, a key factor is learning to adapt.

"Being able to adapt is key. The number of bands I have been in, I have to adapt. So, in Beth Blade's band, I hold back to showcase Beth as its Beth Blade and the Beautiful Disasters. She showcases us, but we must sit back and let her shine. And of course, I can go back to Tigertailz to show off and be as extravagant as I can but working with Beth and Last Great Dreamers was a different type of vibe - and you know you have to adapt. When auditioning for Tigertailz I needed 15 songs. I did the songs and they were happy. I was happy with the idea of fitting in with the band. Its fundamental to learn your parts and know how you fit in - always know what is best for the band. That is fundamental."

Like Berty, I've spent many years on the road. It's something you have to accept if you want to be a success. Berty picks up on this and how hard graft is not just expected but necessary. Without the graft, quite simply – there is no glory.

"I could be going to completely new locations at a drop of a hat. I did an audition about fifteen years ago with lads based in Dumfries, I had just turned eighteen at the time – a band called Dirty Angels. I heard one of their songs on the cover of Classic Rock, went all the way to Dumfries on the National Express and didn't do the gig after all that. But that's normally what happens, you will end up finding out about the bands, then liking the band, being friends of the band, then end up being in the band. This is how it works for me. Networking is an important thing.

There is a band called Drug Dealer Cheerleader. They did a show in the *Gasworks* in Bradford and they started doing some more shows. They had no bass player, so they asked me. I agreed, as an eighteen/nineteen-year-old kid who had barely been out of Yorkshire and been given a tour covering half the UK and my first time properly in London. As a young musician, playing a gig in London was a big deal. The guys who I was playing with had a decade on top of me, so they had a lot more experience – I was like a love shy puppy.

It's very easy to get caught up in the moment, but you learn quickly to deal with the rougher side. I have utmost highs and the lows, but you soon learn to access the situation and make the best of it."

Shooting the breeze with Berty Burton is always inspiring, so I conclude our chat by asking him for some more advice. I mean, if anybody knows - Berty will.

"Try everything and see what works," he says. "Try playing a different style, wear a different outfit – it may work, it may not. Experiment with new shit. As much as people might deny it, nothing is original anymore but make it your own. So, when I still get my attire sorted for Tigertailz, the first half of me looks like a wrestler and I wear flares on my bottom half. It's my style and it's who I am."

Taking to Berty got me thinking about what got me into music in the first place. And like us all, I believe our first gig is a pivotal moment.

I was young and still in short trousers I was taken to Dundee's Caird Hall and saw a band called Big Country. I didn't know what to expect if I'm honest but the sound and sights I witnessed blew me away. It goes without saying I've been a Big Country fan ever since. I've lost count of how many times I have seen them live and lost count of how many times I've walked down the high street listening to Restless Natives, Look Away, One Great Thing, Fields of Fire, The Teacher and Remembrance Day in my earphones and being submerged into this wonderful world. So, what an honour it was chatting to founding member Bruce Watson about what inspired him to get on to that stage and (although he never knew it) change my life.

Bruce tells me, "I went to see the David Essex movies, I was a big cinema goer – and watched Tommy, so that inspired me. Also, bands such as the Alex Harvey Band, Nazareth, who were a big Dunfermline band, and of course the Skids with the Dunfermline link too."

I still love watching bands, but I'm not going as much at all so I look at *YouTube*, look at the new music. There's some really great bands out there."

I talk of passing the baton and ask him about his son Jamie, who is now a member of Big Country and The Skids.

"I didn't really want him to go into it or take my shortcuts, but he picked it up and he was great. Richard Johnson called about the 30th anniversary for one of the Skids albums. 'Can you get a band together, as much of the original line-up as possible?' He asked me. Stuart always had two guitars, double tracked himself so I wasn't sure.

'Your son plays guitar,' he said.

So, Jamie's first gig was with the Skids. He was seventeen and playing T in the Park Festival. Now it's been twelve years with them and Big Country."

Well, as first gig's go, that has got to be one of the best.

In this part, I will focus on two aspects. Firstly behaviour. And secondly the creative process.

Behaviour, you ask. But come on, I'm a rock star. It's all about the bad behaviour, right? People like the bad ass. Look at Axl, Lemmy, Moon. Who wants to be a Cliff Richard when they can be a Cliff Burton? What I'm saying is, have a rock n roll image and a rock-and-roll lifestyle if that is what you choose. Of course, there is nothing wrong with that. I am not here to tell you how to live your life, amigos. What I may politely remind you of though is to protect your brand.

And your brand is insanely precious, valuable and always worth protecting.

Berty Burton talks about the brand to me. "I got into AC/DC because I loved the logo.

Why have KISS been successful for 50 years? After 45 years they still perform that well, they are a brand, but they are great at what they do. I don't care what you think about Kiss I think they are fucking fantastic. The old AC/DC mentality – if it's not broken -don't fix it"

I think of what Sir Burton has to say. I love Iron Maiden, but in truth, did I fall in love with them when I was younger because of Steve Harris's galloping bass or due to Eddie and the logo?

I do what I can to protect my brand. Pete K Mally; comedian, author, presenter, compere is a brand. At one festival that will remain nameless, one of the volunteers mentioned to my boss at the radio station I had a can of beer in my hand while on the stage. To me, this wasn't a problem, but I dealt with it first-hand and in person as I felt she was criticising my brand. As we all know, it can take decades to build a brand and seconds to destroy it.

With that in mind, protect your brand at all costs. Social media platforms are visible for the world to see and your posts will affect your brand, either positively or negatively. I have stopped playing numerous bands on my radio show because I fundamentally disagree with what they are saying on social media. I haven't spoken to them about this – I've just stopped playing them on *my* show. And I don't reckon I am the only one. Think about it for a second. Forget the argument, it's my private page and not on the band page - rubbish. There is no *private* page on the World Wide Web. Rightly or wrongly, this my friends is a fact of life.

I'm not saying do not post anything political or personal – but simply be aware that you have a brand and you are promoting that brand on every post.

As I am typing this, yes on this very day I have seen a post with someone who is a public figure complaining that Marcus Rashford will receive his MBE. All I can think is, 'wow, sour grapes dude.' It looks like, to me anyway that he is aiming for comments claiming he should receive one. For me, his brand is slightly tarnished as he is acting like a petulant child. It's not a major crisis, but he should be aware of his brand and what it represents.

When you are at a gig, your professionalism, your attitude to the venue, attitude to the organisers and mainly the fans will affect your brand's reputation.

"Just treat others like you would want to be treated," Berty Burton states. "Find out your sound guy's name – he/she's going to determine if you are going to sound great or shite, communicate and help out your fellow bands who are sharing the stage. You might be leading the example for the support bands.

It doesn't cost to be nice – be approachable. People will come and speak to me after shows, its great - thanks for chatting to me – if it wasn't because of you I wouldn't be here.

It's very humbling for someone to ask for a photo, or even a signature or a chat.

Chatting to the audience about my dogs. I give the time of day to someone for being human. Having human conversation with fans is invaluable."

Well said, Berty.

So always protect your brand. Or in other words, don't be a dick. Easy, really.

The last section of this chapter, but not the least important is finding your zone. Most literature on the topic of creativity will tell us that finding our own creative space is the way forward. Thomas Edison had his Menlo Park, Roald Dahl had his writing shed, Rob Buller famous saxophonist and most talented man in Cheam has his studio at the end of his garden.

But in reality, space is limited and in many cases if you had space to build a studio, create a shed in which lawnmowers, Christmas decorations and your collection of VHS videos aren't stored or be able to build a studio basement with a pool table, a backline and a beer fridge you probably wouldn't be reading this book.

If you are lucky enough to have a space, however, make it so it breeds creativity. In my man-cave hangs a picture of Bruce Springsteen and Clarence Clemons. Two men I hold in awe and amazement. It is also filled with my Stephen King and Robin Hobb collection, as well as other works of fiction. On the shelves sit biographies and autobiographies of Steven Tyler, Nelson Mandela, Debbie Harry, Andy Kaufman, George Carlin, Slash, Axl Rose and many others. When I feel like giving anything less than 100%, I look at one of the covers and ask myself what they have achieved. What did they bring to the party? And I ask myself should I pass the baton anyway I can. (I have read them too, by the way.)

I asked Karly Jewell where she did her best work.

"Ideas hit me anywhere, like when I'm driving. The bathroom has great acoustics. Although I've got a music room at home, the bathroom is where I write my songs."

Bruce said something similar, and wisely focuses on not so much the 'where' but the atmosphere around. "I can work anywhere where there are no distractions. Not fixed on a place, but I try to remove distractions. I need quietness. The best song writing is when you just allow it to happen and become a conduit. It's just about allowing the thing to be."

The way Massive's Brad's works resonates with the above.

"Usually I can write late at night, where there are no distractions. If I have the house to myself or go for a walk with my headphones and sing to myself. I like peace and quiet when I'm trying to write, I don't like distractions. No spot that I have to be in, as long as I can switch my mind off and focus in on the song."

What is being said here is you do not need to your million-pound soundproof studio to get it done. And just to confirm, Ricky Warwick concurs. And if you've had the pleasure to listen to his music, boy he can write a tune and a half.

"I adhere to the whole thing you can write anywhere. I have three or four guitars and I work and treat it like a job. Usually get up at 6.30, get to the gym for an hour and a half, and pick up the guitar – even if I don't want to. Even if I'm not in the mood. Even if I don't feel it. I go to work and write something. It may be shit. I might write something all week and have nothing, but sometimes the gems come. There's no – 'I've got to be in a cabin' stuff."

Ricky tells me about the experience he had in his friend's cabin. "It was inspiring and beautiful, but instead of being super-creative he just wondered what his kids were up to. He continues, "I read interviews with Nick Cave and David Bowie. Nick Cave puts his suit on and goes down to his basement. The results were huge, that's when I started churning out all the records. That's when I started to treat it with the respect it deserves. I'm not that guy, up until 4am when I have an idea. It's not for everyone, somebody gets inspirational at 4am, but that's not me. The first three or four hours of the day in the morning are the best. A lot of the time the first thing I play or write is great and I start questioning it – that was too easy. "

Imogen from Novustory talks about her writing and creative spaces.

"Generally, I write when I'm sad," she tells me. "I write well when I feel emotionally in turmoil. Happy sounding songs I write always have a dark undertone. I started in my bedroom, then me and James start using a shed. The next step, we set up shop in a small studio and write in there, set up a mini keyboard. Now we've made a live room.

I've got a baby grand piano," she tells me as her eyes light up with excitement. "There's something so special about a real piano. I feel really connected to the instrument. I'm twenty-five and am playing a baby grand piano. It's like an out-of-body experience.

It feels nice; I feel fancy. I feel like a fraud. You spend so much time to get to a certain level, then you get there and feel like fraud. I feel like I've duped someone to get it."

Again, Emma from False Hearts focusing more on the act of creating than the space that's required. It's a common thread and reflects the philosophy that the where is less of a priority than the how and the why.

"My side is the melody and the lyrics, so it comes last in our process. I listen to the guide track, get the vibe, then the story forms in my head.

I listen to it in by ear, it goes around in my head. Some songs it takes a couple minutes, some a couple of days. It depends on how it flows.

That's one thing that surprised me, I didn't have any idea about the music writing process. Sometimes it can be so natural, it's amazing to know that sometimes if you trust enough that other people might like it and it tells a story it comes together."

Verity White and I talk about the intimacy of writing and the emotivity of the process. She writes with her husband Alex, although they write separately. After talking to these masters of creativity, I fully understand this. Verity tells me where she writes, apart from away from her husband. "I work best sat in the house; I have a gin shed. I don't drink gin constantly," she laughs. "And a vinyl room, which are my two happy spaces. We work separately as the music and the creative process is so raw and emotive."

On sight of the gin shed and the vinyl room, Verity has very much made these spaces her own. To me, an outsider it appears soaked with comfort, inspiration and good vibes. And yes, gin.

Nic Wastell tells me a story that tickles me pink, about the creating process and using your own space for writing. After informing me he uses a place in his house because "my missus hates my music," he tells me about a Sir Paul McCartney interview that he once read. "Paul McCartney," he says, "once told a reporter that he wrote the rockers in the day, but the ballads at night. Because, when the kids have gone to bed, he had to sing really quietly."

He continues, "I've always written on an old acoustic. If it worked on the acoustic guitar, it works. You soon learn what it was like through a *Marshall*. I used to sit, wait until people went to bed and do my work."

Marc and Slyder from The Last Great Dreamers also tell me about their creative process.

"My kitchens got tiles, so it's got great acoustics, so I play in there but in the writing phase I always need privacy. I need it to be complete before I can share it, so privacy and quiet is important to me."

"Yeah," Marc laughs. "Most of my writing is done in the kitchen, between ten o'clock and midnight, me and an acoustic guitar. One of the kids will bang on the floor - Dad shut up I'm trying to sleep."

Marc has recently built a little studio space for his creative output. Again, it harbours that creative energy. He tells me it is needed as there are six of them in the house. It's the place he can find quiet.

The song writing process can be a precarious one.

"I think about songs anywhere. My phone is littered with voice messages with bit of tunes, melodies. Sometimes I have some notes in my phone that make no sense," Slyder tells me, "I had a song dream recently. I had two songs from it. I wake up with the melody. I woke up and got my acoustic out, worked out the melody and chorus and got it down. It's bizarre, *Lunacy Lady*, I remember thinking of that at work. I was decorating a health centre. Once it's in your head you've got to get it down.

You always get the inspiration two minutes before you stop writing. Suddenly get an inspiration."

Marc agrees. "Yup, you sit down, mess around with some ideas, think - this is terrible, play a couple of minutes. Just then in that last minute it comes to you. Unbearably sometimes, just before you must go somewhere or when the kids will walk in just as I found it.

Then it's gone, back to the ether and gone."

It's great talking about the creative process and one take-away is it takes patience, hard-work, usually quiet and sometimes a lot of frustration. Even for the best of them.

Since 2020 was such a crazy year, the lack of gigs for both performers and audience members was painful. Myke Gray soon made it easier by rolling out a live stream that imitated the live experience brilliantly. For that performance he recruited Daniel Byrne from Revival Black.

Revival Black's debut album *Step in Line* is already touted as a rock classic. A band who know what hard work is and have the results to prove it. Daniel is their frontman and his vocals are sublime.

Myke Gray, guitarist formerly with Skin, Red White & Blues, Schism, and Jagged Edge has now formed out a majestic solo career. Myke is a hero of mine in both the music he emits and his exceptional work ethic. I first saw Myke at Donington Monsters of Rock in 1994 and then at Hyde Park Calling, twenty years later. Since then I had the pleasure of catching him twice in 2018 and I am an avid fan of his recent released material, *Shades of Gray.*

Knowing Myke's commitment to his art, when I heard he would be performing an online show, I didn't think it would be a show that he did what he could. "That'll do," wouldn't be a phrase that comes from Myke's mouth. Everything he delivers is of the highest quality and his online stream was no exception. So, I caught up with Myke - and Daniel Byrne, the young singer from the upcoming and utterly brilliant Revival Black, who sang for Myke in this streamed sensation.

"It's not about the girls, the money or the fame. For me, it's all about the music," Myke tells me. "Many guitar players have influenced me over the years, but the ones that have a special place in my heart would be Eddie Van Halen Randy Rhoads, Jimi Hendrix, Michael Schenker, Stevie Ray Vaughan and Angus Young. The effect that all of these players have on me is indescribable. "Hearing them play creates an emotion of pure joy."

"I think music at its best is inspirational and often the people it inspires the most are other musicians. As an example Bob Dylan wrote All Along the Watchtower, a fantastically emotive song in its raw form but Hendrix took it and developed it something different and made it his own. When you hear the first two notes, it's simply unbelievable."

I asked Myke and Dan who they received the baton from and what it meant for them to receive such a gift.

"Fish," Dan replies instantly. "He is the biggest musical influence in my musical life. I was about six years old and was force fed Fish and Marillion, which was amazing. That was my first exposure, at a three-day convention of Fish and Marillion," he laughs.

Dan shows me one of the coolest photos ever. One of himself, a very young boy indeed, with the Scottish Hibernian fan himself. I love it that this young lead singer has his roots firmly in gratitude for those who inspired him.

"When I see Fish now, I tear up when he plays certain songs, it's the emotion," he tells me. "I'm lucky. I'm from a family who is very supportive of what I do."

Myke tells me of his introduction to the music he now gifts to the world.

"The Sex Pistols were the first band that musically spoke to me, i was drawn to the anger and energy. I remember hearing *Pretty Vacant* for the first time and it caught my imagination. But hearing the first Van Halen was life changing for me. From that moment on I knew exactly what I wanted to do with my life.

Listening to Myke Gray's enthusiasm about his rock music education would inspire anybody to go into a music shop and pick up a guitar. I tell him this, so I will tell you, the reader this also. I would love to see *An Evening with Mr Gray*, playing his songs and talking about his musical journey. Fascinating.

Dan talks to me about his band Revival Black and his work with Myke.

"Revival Black's *Step in Line*, is a full-on album, enclosed in the rock genre. You pour your heart into a song that may not sound that emotional, putting what you're thinking into words and making it poetic is important.

I'm not someone who goes out drinking and taking drugs, to me rock n roll is emotion. I love the rock n roll community; these festivals and these shared experiences is almost as important as the music itself.

There's a fixation to make sure everything is perfect. It's an escape for the audience and us as well. It's like prayer – like a church. Everyone is together and has a shared experience. The experience of thing going wrong live builds character and you can take something from that too.

That's transferrable. You can take when something goes wrong on stage and take that to life. It's key to personal growth."

Dan is 23 and I suspect is a Jedi-master. Young, kind, talented and wise - the dude is a true inspiration. I ask him about being asked to sing for the Myke Gray gig.

"They were wearing underpants that are older than me in that group," he laughs. "I am very new to this myself. You learn so much about people, being in a band. Not only do you learn people management, there's a certain confidence you pick up. I am now more fully equipped – these are skills I have developed. Two years ago, I wouldn't say boo to a goose, speak to when spoken to. I didn't even ask for people or money, didn't want to put them out. You learn a lot. Working with Myke and the band was an honour and an experience that can't ever be bought. What am I doing taken up this space? I have doubts, but the inclusivity and the acceptance has been the nicest thing I've been a part of. The people we are surrounded by are the nicest people in the world. The community is incredible. I was shitting myself, because Myke is such a legend. I did backing vocals to *Shades of Gray*, so when he asked me to sing, I couldn't physically say how much that meant to me.

There's a certain way how Myke works, and for me I can learn from that. We are both very critical, with attention to detail. People ask in everyday life why am I so picky, but when you earn something from the music, that one note may make a different sound and sometimes you have to be that picky because that's the difference between good and excellent."

I ask both artists about the reason they choose to work so damn hard. "It is about creating a legacy," Myke says. "My songs are bigger than me, my body of work will outlive me."

Dan shadows the reasons. "It's not so much about what I want to be remembered by but the work. I would much rather have a song that people can remember than for example what stunt Dan did that time. My work and my contribution are so important. If I could influence anyone, if anybody can take up singing because of me, that would mean so much for me. I'm a guitarist by trade but I sing because we couldn't get a singer. I sounded about as good as David Coverdale's big toes," he laughs. "I still technically sing wrong, but I was in that position. I couldn't sing so I learnt to sing."

Myke concludes about the writing process "Inspiration comes from many places, sometimes you spend days, weeks and months working on something but nothing feels right but then something materialises and you wonder where did that come from? It can even come from picking up a different guitar. I wrote *Stand Up For Rock & Roll* the moment I got my first *Gibson SG*. An idea can come straight to you, other times there is a lot of writing and re-writing and developing. Writing is time-consuming but it is driven by the desire to make each song as good as it can possibly be, and even then a song is open to someone else's interpretation."

The attitude from these two masters in their field is sublime. In the early parts of this section of the book I talked about brand and reputation. Do yourself a favour and check out the work of Revival Black and Myke Gray. Both are awesome, both are professional and both tackle everything they do with the highest of standards. A pair of champions.

I salute you gentlemen

This book has been about motivation, not giving up and about being influenced, then carving out a path of your own. So, how happy was I when I caught up with lead singer Nathan James from rock outfit Inglorious. I've been a fan of Inglorious for a long time now and been a fan of Nathan himself since I first met him. For me, watching a band storm that stage is amazing. But seeing that same band stand in the crowd watching other bands on the same bill with clear admiration is priceless. I stood with

Nathan, watching Foreigner at Ramblin' Man. I've stood with him at Stonedeaf Festival watching Glenn Hughes.

I ask him about this baton and who he grabbed it from.

"My influences have always been singers and frontmen. I'm obsessed with David Coverdale, Glenn Hughes, Paul Rodgers, Freddie Mercury, Axl Rose; people with unique incredible instruments. Freddie, he's the king. The most eccentric wonderful creature who has ever walked the planet," he tells me. "Glenn Hughes is brilliant. I was obsessed as a kid, with him and I wanted to push myself until one day I could sing like him. I used to listen to Burn - and wish I could sing these notes one day.

It's amazing and that's the most interesting thing about music, we are so heavily inspired, I mean no-one truly is original. Maybe David Bowie; apart from that there is no one 100 percent original. We take things from the previous generation. I clearly wear my references on my sleeve, you can hear the Coverdale in my voice."

Hughes, Coverdale, Mercury. We talk about these three timeless voices for a while. Three singers who have given the gift of their voice to the world and influenced millions. Nathan James being one of them.

"They will die one day; it's really shit but they will. But if we can keep it going, we pass it on. That's what we are doing. When Glenn Hughes dies, someone must be the voice of rock," Nathan says. His smile is contagious when he quickly adds, "I don't want him to die, obviously. I love him with all my heart. Love him and he is a friend, but it is inevitable someday.

But I would love some kid to look at me how I look at him. I wouldn't exist without Glenn Hughes and David Coverdale.

I would love people to call me – the best rock singer in Britain. For one time, even if it's for a fucking week." He laughs.

Nathan and I talk about music, festivals and heroes of ours. The conversation again goes to Freddie Mercury. I show Nathan my forehead as it is the same as Freddie's. It must be a Zanzibar thing.

"Can you image someone like Freddie's sharp tongue on social media," Nathan laughs. But he has a most serious point. "This is the worst thing about this, the social media can be horrible. What I constantly think of my heroes is that I'm so jealous that no one could instantly comment of their goings on. If you are telling me that Axl Rose would have been a social media dream in the eighties, you are talking shit.

David Coverdale changed his band a million times and only official magazines mentioned it, not people at home. So, I'm very jealous of that for that reason."

Nathan wears his heart on his sleeve and his talk about social media is priceless. If anyone knows the double-edged sword of this new world, it is Mr James. I, myself have heard comments about Nathan. As you dig deeper, (not by much) you realise that most of these comments are made by those who have never met him. As many of you who know me know, I don't tolerate ego very well. For me, and as the book previously states, I don't think there is a space in this world for pre-madonnas, ego and arrogance. There are bands (who will remain unnamed) I find their attitude or change in attitude displeasing so I will just put them to one side and wish them the best. Believe me when I tell you I have met Nathan on several occasions and every single time (offstage, onstage, backstage) he is one of the warmest, kindest people out there. And talented. Very talented, indeed.

"I'm so proud to be part of the rock community, I think its accepting and full of kind people – but there is always an exception and unfortunately, we saw it. The homophobic and racist side. I think, what is wrong with you? Keyboard warriors. Who can sit at home and thinking their comment is okay? You can't say you're supporting the rock community and be a person who's not accepting of people."

We talk about standards and how high standards need to be the benchmark.

"I could only work with the best, I've been so spoiled," Nathan says. "Every job I've had with a band. For example, the Michael Jackson *Thriller* musical, where I was there for a year, we had the most insane talent, legendary musicians for example, Gabor Dornyei on drums. I've done a jam once with Steve Vai, I've been over in Japan with Uli Jon Roth, I've worked with the best. I did Ginger Baker's last ever recording in Abbey Road. So now I am at the point of my career I want to surround myself with the best. I don't want to fizzle out. I want to grow everyday – just like Glenn."

Nathan's enthusiasm about his craft is contagious.

He continues, "it's no secret I have had a few members of my band, but all of them are without doubt the best musicians in the UK at that time, so when you think of it like that I surrounded myself with greatness.

Hard work is what people fear, especially the younger generation. I didn't wake up one day with a big voice and an understanding of music."

I dig a bit deeper about the future. Nathan tells me about the new Inglorious album and his excitement about going on the road again. "I can't wait to get out with the first album with this line up, although it seems ridiculous as we've been together for two years. These guys have a lot to prove. This band always is about great musicianship and these guys aren't scared of that at all. They've grabbed it by the horns and written a wicked album with me, and we have had a great producer. It's very exciting to show. Think Inglorious on acid. The highest level of performance. And happiness. I've never been so happy; the fans will see that – it filters down. This time, I'm happier, I love and trust and respect them all. We all know our positions. We all want to be the best that we can be. The best guitarist they can be, the best bass player they can be, the best drummer they can be, and I'll be the best singer I can be."

This book is ultimately about why we do what we do. The *why* should motivate you, push you to create, show your art to the world and make the globe a better place. Talking to Nathan, as always - inspires me and moves me forward to create. I finish off our conversation asking him with all the hard graft, the dedication and the pitfalls – *why* he does what he does.

"The fact that you can watch all these bands at a festival, who you adore, is mind-blowing. We love playing to all these people but sharing the stage with other bands is incredible. We are fans first of this music. I feel so lucky that I've got to see so many amazing people. One weekend we played Sweden on the Friday and the Download Festival on the Sunday and watched Ozzy and Zakk Wylde from the pit twice in a weekend. I mean, what an experience."

Foreigner are a band that I have payed fifty, sixty, eighty quid to go and see, and the fact that we are getting paid to share the stage with them is incredible. It was magical watching Foreigner at Ramblin Man Fair. And my whole family was there, it was an amazing thing to share with them. And its moments like that, it makes it worthwhile.

These are special moments. It's at times like that you are on cloud nine."

He laughs. "I had a piss next to Nikki Sixx at Download. I mean, really.

There's always a massive comedown after a festival season. You've seen all your mates, met your idols, played to thousands of people, the weather is usually good - so it's a real comedown after that. But I feel so lucky that I get to do it again, and still learn. I'm always learning.

We still learn, at the Graspop Festival, there was Whitesnake, Def Leppard and Kiss on the same stage we were playing on. You learn so much. You learn from every single band. I mean I was taking notes on how to be like those legends. These incredible performers. I feel very blessed to do this for a living now."

Nathan laughs again. He follows it by saying, "the fucking weirdest one for me was when David Coverdale walked offstage during a drum solo, pointed at me and said, 'Nathan, darling.' I honestly, screamed like a little girl. I couldn't contain it. He fucking knew my name. We were in a car crash the day before. He mentioned it. He asked if we were okay. What a gentleman. I try to be like that with people that I meet."

Again, I re-instate a previous comment I made. Every Inglorious gig I've been to, the fans leave joyous for two reasons. One, Inglorious have just kicked their ass. Two, if the fans have wanted to talk to Nathan and the band, they have had the opportunity and were thoroughly pleased that they did.

Nathan continues, "I could stand at the side of the stage, but I want to be in with the crowd, I am a fan first. Listening to that massive sound.

When you see your family out there, singing along – it's so special. They worked their asses of so we could pursue our dreams, so it is so special to invite them. Its moments like this I get to pay them back.

As much as Glenn and David are my heroes, my parents are amazing. They gave me a great work ethic; they know how to graft. I've picked up the hard work ethics. I've had people knocking me down, but I always get back up.

I' m not letting them win. I've worked too hard to let some keyboard warrior tell me what to do with my day.

I'm never ever giving up, I'm currently loving it, love being in the band, love it."

Wise words, Mr Nathan James. Rock-and-Roll, and Resilience. Can I just add here that at the Stonedeaf Festival, I was on the stage on the DJ decks when Inglorious were performing and the energy, talent and above all joy oozing from every pore was beautiful. I left the stage a better man than I entered it.

Last but certainly not least in this journey of catching up with inspirational superstars, I chatted to two members of possibly the coolest family in the UK. Kyle Lamley is the driving force of Theia. Theia are one of my favourite bands out there. Their music is right up my street and watching this three-piece on stage reminds you that life is great. Their energy, their charisma, and their connections within the band and to the audience is second to none.

Only in the Lamley household would Kyle's Dad Keith realise that Theia wouldn't get any air play on some radio stations without a label, so he created one. WDFD.

Yes, you heard that correctly. The answer is there when you look for it, right? I would like to make a correction here. They are not as previously stated 'possibly the coolest family'. They *are* the coolest family. I asked them where the baton came from. Who influenced the Lamleys? Kyle answers, "the first influences from me were all from Dad. T.Rex, Slade, Alice Cooper. Dad had a couple of VHS videos and the one of Alice Cooper was out of this world. I loved it. To me it was all about the persona, larger than live personas. The people were fascinating to me."

Keith agrees, "for me, Noddy Holder, Marc Bolan, again Alice Cooper - all real characters. I listened to my dad's stuff, The Seekers which proceeded the New Seekers. I remember sitting cross legged listening to T.Rex for the first time at a friend's house and they blew me away.

But again, for me I was there for the 70s, it was the glam stuff. It was about the visuals, these people were different, they were special."

I asked Keith about WDFD. A record label that showcases an amazing rota of bands and is renowned for its professional, yet ethical stance in this industry.

Keith tells me, "a radio station wouldn't take tracks from unsigned bands, so I set up a label. It seemed stupidly easy to get around a stupid rule. I never intended to take on more bands, it was just for Theia, it just grew." He laughs, "I really love Theia's music, thankfully."

"As I have grown older," Kyle muses. "I know I am still a young musician in the grand scheme of things, but I've learned a lot of lessons. I've been doing this for ten years.

I now understand that many fish are trying to swim in one little bowl, maybe we can look in another bowl, or maybe we are looking out of the fishbowl, looking at the ocean. There is a new world out there and new ways to capture people. If only I can get off my arse and figure it out," he laughs. "There is always a mountain to climb, it's just recognising that and focusing on it."

I ask him about Theia. Was it a deliberate move to involve the family?

"Theia has been organic from day one, Theia is my band. I always wanted to play the Star and Garter, that was my aim. When we did, Dad was there, carrying gear and making sure we were allowed in the venue. My brother has carried more gear than me. It was never a plan to keep it in the family, a Von Trapp affair, it was purely organic. It was a natural progression. We are a tight family. I've got two older sisters, and my brother (who is now drummer in Theia) and my amazing mum and we have all been involved in the band. That's just what we do – we look after each other."

Keith, or Sir Keith of Lamley as he is warmly known in the business continues, "I would be humbled if anybody saw us as an inspiration. It can be a double-edged sword though, it's not my natural skillset. I was in a band years ago and we knocked our head against a brick wall. I've got no magical powers. Its hugely supportive to have the family bond but you do also learn and have to be able to re-assess. The music scene is at a weird stage. The truth is, it's tough to break through and you have to be honest and ask if there's something we are not doing.

There is huge pride in the band. I do love Theia and the band gel well together. But it's frustrating because people love the band, but its translating that into why it doesn't propel you more. Yes, you want people to feel good but in terms of making it a career it must translate into something bigger. If you are trying to make a career out of it, you must try to take it up a notch. And that's not easy."

Kyle agrees. "It's the driving force behind it. The connection is real. But I would enjoy it just as much, even more perhaps if we were headlining Reading and Leeds. Regardless of what we wear; jeans, t-shirts, suits, ringmasters' outfits - we give the same amount of effort, care and dedication at every performance. It matters who you have around you. You need good teams around you. You need the infrastructure There has got to be something real for people to latch onto, it's not just the music and the songs – you have to capture everything these days because of social media."

The social media world, as previously noted is a tricky one sometimes to navigate. Keith's wisdom slices through it like a knife through butter. "The circle we operate in is wonderful but relatively small, so if you are going to be a dickhead it's there to all to see."

"Absolutely" Kyle agrees. "From a bands side I have always been wary on posting opinions. Just be careful how you text, texts read differently from those reading them. My dad taught me that when I was younger. This cancel culture we live in – we are under intense scrutiny, people will scroll, find something and look back. You have to be careful."

Talking to all of those people has taught me loads. But mainly, it has reminded me that the world is not all doom, gloom, work and no play, pesky viruses, greedy politicians and problems in the EU.

The world is full of creative juices and it is a fantastic place to swim in.

This is the time I should write a witty and inspiring paragraph on the reasons why we should go and be creative. I could mention how you will cleanse the soul-set or increase the activity of the right hemisphere of the brain or discuss the increased productivity of dopamine.

But I won't.

I will simply ask you to look at the people who have carved the path before you.

It is now your turn.

Place this book neatly on your book shelve, or if it's a Kindle turn it off.

And Go Create. And make this world even better.

Big love

Pete K Mally

2020

To all the contributors of this book, I give you my heartfelt thanks. For me, it's been a true honour.

For Keith and Kyle Lamley, Daniel Byrne, Myke Gray, Nathan James, Bruce Watson, Berty Burton, Marc

Valentine, Slyder Smith, Emma Hodgson, Ricky Warwick, Karly Jewell, Imogen Rosemary, Verity White, Bruce Dickinson, Nic Wastell and Brad Marr.

THANK YOU. Not just for your time but for your body of work. It's a gift.

Check out:

MASSIVE – https://www.massiveoz.com/

THE LAST GREAT DREAMERS - https://www.lastgreatdreamers.com/

NOVUSTORY - http://novustory.reverbnation.com/

KARLY JEWELL - https://karlyjewell.com/

WAYWARD SONS - https://www.waywardsonsband.com/site/

VERITY WHITE - https://www.veritywhite.com/

FALSE HEARTS - https://www.falsehearts.com/

THEIA - https://theiauk.com/

WDFD RECORDS - https://wdfd-records.com/

TIGERTAILZ - http://www.tigertailz.co.uk/

INGLORIOUS - http://inglorious.com/

RICKY WARWICK - https://www.nuclearblast.de/en/label/music/band/about/4026616.ricky-warwick.html

MYKE GRAY - https://www.mykegray.rocks/

REVIVAL BLACK - http://tmrbandmanagement.com/tmr-roster/revival-black/

Printed in Great Britain
by Amazon